T0318512

Cambridge Elements ≡

Elements in Philosophy and Logic
edited by
Bradley Armour-Garb
SUNY Albany
Frederick Kroon
The University of Auckland

RELEVANCE LOGIC

Shay Allen Logan
Kansas State University

CAMBRIDGE
UNIVERSITY PRESS

Shaftesbury Road, Cambridge CB2 8EA, United Kingdom

One Liberty Plaza, 20th Floor, New York, NY 10006, USA

477 Williamstown Road, Port Melbourne, VIC 3207, Australia

314–321, 3rd Floor, Plot 3, Splendor Forum, Jasola District Centre, New Delhi – 110025, India

103 Penang Road, #05–06/07, Visioncrest Commercial, Singapore 238467

Cambridge University Press is part of Cambridge University Press & Assessment, a department of the University of Cambridge.

We share the University's mission to contribute to society through the pursuit of education, learning and research at the highest international levels of excellence.

www.cambridge.org
Information on this title: www.cambridge.org/9781009536172

DOI: 10.1017/9781009227773

First published 2024

A catalogue record for this publication is available from the British Library.

ISBN 978-1-009-53617-2 Hardback
ISBN 978-1-009-22775-9 Paperback
ISSN 2516-418X (online)
ISSN 2516-4171 (print)

Relevance Logic

Elements in Philosophy and Logic

DOI: 10.1017/9781009227773
First published online: March 2024

Shay Allen Logan
Kansas State University

Author for correspondence: Shay Allen Logan, salogan@ksu.edu

Abstract: Relevance logics are a misunderstood lot. Despite being the subject of intense study for nearly a century, they remain maligned as too complicated, too abstruse, or too silly to be worth learning much about. This Element aims to dispel these misunderstandings. By focusing on the weak relevant logic B, the discussion provides an entry point into a rich and diverse family of logics. Also, it contains the first-ever textbook treatment of quantification in relevance logics, as well as an overview of the cutting edge on variable sharing results and a guide to further topics in the field.

Keywords: relevance logic, nonclassical logic, entailment, theory building, stratified semantics

ISBNs: 9781009536172 (HB), 9781009227759 (PB), 9781009227773 (OC)
ISSNs: 2516-418X (online), 2516-4171 (print)

Contents

1 Introduction

Logic is the study of inference. Not inference generally, but good inference. And not good inference generally, but inferences of the very best sort – inference, that is, that is wholly and entirely unimpeachable.

There's more to say than this. A plausible starting point is the trio of restrictions mentioned in Beall and Restall (2005): logic must be necessary, normative, and formal. These criteria, in turn, have been criticized and other criteria have been examined as well. But even if we pause at the level of wholly and entirely unimpeachable inference, there's reason to think that logic, as traditionally practiced, doesn't meet the bar it places for itself.

At the heart of the problem we have in mind is the issue of relevance. In one of the most (in?)famous passages in the history of relevance logics, Anderson and Belnap present the sort of worry I have in mind as follows:

> Imagine, if you can, a situation as follows. A mathematician writes a paper on Banach spaces, and after proving a couple of theorems he concludes with a conjecture. As a footnote to the conjecture, he writes: "In addition to its intrinsic interest, this conjecture has connections with other parts of mathematics which might not immediately occur to the reader. For example, if the conjecture is true, then the first order functional calculus is complete; whereas if it is false, then it implies that Fermat's last conjecture is correct." The editor replies that the paper is obviously acceptable, but he finds the final footnote perplexing; he can see no connection whatever between the conjecture and the "other parts of mathematics," and none is indicated in the footnote. So the mathematician replies, "Well, I was using 'if . . . then -' and 'implies' in the way that logicians have claimed I was: the first order functional calculus is complete, and necessarily so, so anything implies that fact – and if the conjecture is false it is presumably impossible, and hence implies anything. And if you object to this usage, it is simply because you have not understood the technical sense of 'if . . . then -' worked out so nicely for us by logicians." And to this the editor counters: "I understand the technical bit all right, but it is simply not correct. In spite of what most logicians say about us, the standards maintained by this journal require that the antecedent of an 'if . . . then -' statement must be relevant to the conclusion drawn. And you have given no evidence that your conjecture about Banach spaces is relevant either to the completeness theorem or to Fermat's conjecture."
> . . . the editor's point is that though the technical meaning is clear, it is simply not the same as the meaning ascribed to "if . . . then -" in the pages of his journal. Furthermore, he has put his finger precisely on the difficulty: "to argue from the necessary truth of A to if B then A is simply to commit a fallacy of relevance. The fancy that relevance is irrelevant to validity strikes us as ludicrous, and we therefore make an attempt to explicate the notion of relevance of A to B." (Anderson & Belnap, 1975, p. 17ff)

This passage has gone in for a lot of criticism over the years (see e.g. Hanson [1989], who in turn points to the earlier Bennett [1969] as having already dealt with the matter), but it seems to capture something that has at least a whiff of plausibility to it: irrelevant inferences don't seem to be wholly and entirely unimpeachable. Or, at the very least, those who make them aren't thereby doing something we oughtn't get mad at them for having done. This is a (perhaps surmountable) strike against logics that admit such irrelevancies.

For now at least, let's take that as given. The problem one immediately encounters is that it's one thing to say one wants a logic that doesn't admit irrelevancies and it's a different thing entirely to say what, exactly, an irrelevancy is, and it's yet another thing altogether to say what it means for a logic as a whole to avoid them. The little we *can* say is pretty well summed up by what I've elsewhere called "Bimbó's Dictum" (see Bimbó, 2007, p. 729) that "An implication is relevant if the antecedent and the consequent are appropriately related." Presumably, then, a logic is relevant if all its implications are.

This is, one has to admit, not much to go on. It's nonetheless been gone on, and the going's been quite good. The sheer variety of different interpretations one might give of "relevance" has left the field wide open for development. The result has been a veritable alphabet soup of formal systems delivered (even in the canonical publications of the field; see Anderson and Belnap [1975], Anderson, Belnap, and Dunn [1992], and Routley, Plumwood, Meyer, and Brady [1982]) piping hot from wherever it is that good logics go when they die. This much is good. But one still wants – and finds oneself criticized by one's peers for being short on – motivation for the work. Ross Brady puts it as follows:

> The problem for relevant logics is that there are far too many of them and, as such, there is a lack of definition in the concept of relevance. If we take relevance as meaning relatedness, which is its immediately intuitive concept, this is, by itself, not a suitable concept upon which to base a logic as it is too vague. (Brady, 2017b, p. 758)

This problem might seem to be a rather serious one for those looking to study the class of logics at hand. But it turns out to be mostly an advertising problem. This was noted quite early on in the development of these systems: "[T]he name 'relevant logics', or 'relevance logic', is not entirely satisfactory – perhaps even, to lodge a much stronger claim, unfortunate – since the name tends to suggest, wrongly, that relevance is of the essence, instead of being a peripheral concern" (Routley et al., 1982, p. x).

But if relevance is peripheral, then what's at the heart? Several answers have been given. The one I offer and defend in what follows is not, in fact, new. It builds on the work of Urquhart, Fine, and Slaney in the first place, but also on a good bit of other work that we'll be citing along the way.[1] What follows, as the preceding should make clear, is the presentation of one thread of research in what's a rather rich tapestry of logico-philosophical work. I will, as befits the presentation of such a thing, be a bit dogmatic about it. But before I stoop to dogmatism, I'll exhort the reader to "not let the [author] grind them down."[2] You are – or are perhaps on the road to becoming – logicians. And to be a logician is to enjoy a kind of unfettered freedom unheard of by those not quite so good at following made-up rules. This freedom is not to be infringed upon by any mere book, and less yet one by me. Better minds than mine said it thus:

> Logic is not a closed shop, and the business of logicians, their elegant and miserable codifications and logical principles, are just as much open to crit-icism and discussion and just as little settleable by the weight of numbers or democratic vote (whether among present or past philosophers), or by histor-ical track record, as philosophical ones and scientific ones. Logicians should no more allow themselves to be browbeaten by tradition than philosophers or scientists. (Routley et al., 1982, p. 159)

2 The Philosophical Picture

We investigate the world around us. We learn and we study and we figure things out. These are among the most human things we do. And, while we're rarely successful in doing so, we aim to do so exhaustively – to find ourselves able to say, about the things we study, all the things there are to say. In service to such an aim, we follow a procedure that Jc Beall has described as follows:

> [O]nce she has identified her target phenomenon (about which she aims to give the true and as-complete-as-possible theory), the task of the theorist is twofold:
> - gather the truths about the target phenomenon
> - construct the right closure relation to "complete" the true theory – to give as full or complete a true theory as the phenomenon allows. Beall (2018, p. 3)

Thus not only are we investigators and learners and studiers and figure-out-ers; we're also *theory-builders*. But what exactly *counts* as a theory?

I need to be completely clear about this right now at the start of things: "the-ory" is, in what follows, a primitive term. It will remain undefined in much the same way as "world" remains undefined in Kripke's possible worlds semantics for modal logic.[3] But just as with possible worlds semantics, so also here there

---

[1] The main works I have in mind, though, are Urquhart (1972), Fine (1974), and Slaney (1990).
[2] To paraphrase Atwood (2006).
[3] See Kripke (1963) or Fitting and Mendelsohn (2012).

are intuitions to be pumped. To pump them properly, one ought to have the thought that theories are "fully fleshed out" sets of sentences.

We've now reached the heart of the matter. What we'll be studying in this Element is how to answer the questions that the discussion so far should naturally give rise to, namely what exactly does it mean for a set of sentences to be "fully fleshed out"? What does it take, that is, for a set of sentences to be a theory? It's worth noting that we don't ask these questions out of idle intellectual curiosity. We ask them because the answers shed light on what it is we're doing when we do those most human things we do – investigate, study, figure things out.

Of course, that might not be what you *thought* this Element was going to be about. The title, after all, was "Relevance Logic," and as discussed in the introduction, this was historically something investigated with an eye toward, well, relevance. But the best case to be made for relevance logics as *logics* is to see them as logics in the way Beall uses the word. Logic, on Beall's view (2018, p. 3) is "the formal entailment relation that plays the role of universal closure relation – or universal basement-level closure relation."

The idea, roughly, is this: there are myriad theory-building practices. Each is equipped with its own story about what it takes for a set of sentences to count as a theory. Corresponding to any such story there is a closure relation – the relation that holds between a set of sentences Γ and a sentence B when B is in the theory Γ generates. In this context "logic" as Beall uses the word is "the relation on top of which all [such] closure relations ... are built" Beall (2018, p. 4). It is, if you like, the ur-closure-relation among closure relations.

Since "universal basement-level closure relation" isn't the only thing one might mean by "logic," we should say a bit about what's appealing about this way of using the word. To begin, note that as Beall has pointed out in a variety of places, using "logic" in this particular way leaves us with an account of logic that has most of the features we'd want – it's universal (because the basement-level closure relation is ipso facto at play in every other closure relation), it's topic neutral (because it works in all theories, no matter the topic), and it's "intransgressible" in the sense that violating logic will always result in violating whatever local closure relation you'd meant to follow.

Here's another nice feature of using "logic" in this way. Suppose we encounter someone who thinks we ought to use "logic" in some other way. Say, for example, that this person wants to say that logic is the study of those arguments that always transmit truth from premise to conclusion. There's nothing wrong, to be sure, with using "logic" in this way. But one should note that before one can actually spell out what "logic" in this sense amounts to, one needs to give a *theory* of truth. And this theory of truth should actually be a theory. So logic in the sense Beall uses the word – and in the sense we'll be using it here – comes first, and it comes first whether you call it "logic" or not.

So much for overview. The way we'll go about actually studying the basement-level closure relation is by building models. The models we give will be models of spaces of theories. And they will be models of spaces of theories that track (among other things) the ways we can combine theories. In this regard, it's important to make a distinction between two ways we might combine theories that is made quite forcefully in the following passage due to John Slaney:

> Bodies of information [note: Slaney uses "body of information" in much the same way I use "theory"] may be used in more than one way.... There is intuitively a difference between using information to tell you how the world stands and using it to tell you how you may reason. That is, you may treat it as a guide to the facts or as a source of inference tickets. A good analogy comes from computation theory: as von Neumann pointed out, one and the same series of symbols can function as program or as data to suit the occasion; as program it operates on input much as a proof operates on its premises, while as data itself it may be the input to or output from other operations. The distinction being sketched is not quite the traditional one between "laws" and "facts," for the difference resides neither in the propositions themselves nor in the information they convey but in the use to which they are put in one context or another. Slaney (1990, pp. 74–75)

Intuitively, for each of Slaney's ways of *using* theories there is, for each theory t, a function from theories to theories. The first function corresponds to the function that maps each theory s to the theory we get by combining s with t while taking t "as a guide to the facts." The second function corresponds to the function that maps each theory s to the theory we get by combining s with t while taking t "as a source of inference tickets." One expects to capture this by giving models in which one has the following sorts of *binary* functions:

$\langle t, s \rangle \mapsto$ the theory we get by combining s with t while taking t to be
      "a guide to the facts"

$\langle t, s \rangle \mapsto$ the theory we get by combining s with t while taking t to be
      "a source of inference tickets"

The difference between these two ways of combining theories is also, I think, mirrored in the different behaviors of the Tortoise and Achilles in Carroll's famous parable (see Carroll [1895]). The story there (taking a few interpretive liberties to help our cause) is roughly this: The Tortoise and Achilles are talking. The subject isn't important. What matters is this: they've agreed that "A"

and "*A* entails *Z*" are true. Achilles is ready to conclude that "*Z*" is true. The Tortoise, on the other hand, contends that "*A*" and "*A* entails *Z*" aren't, on their own, enough to get us to *Z*. What's needed, he convinces Achilles to say, is an additional fact that we'll call *C*:

> "*A*" and "*A* entails *Z*" together entail "*Z*".

Achilles and the Tortoise again find themselves agreeing: "*A*," "*A* entails *Z*," and "*C*" are, they both admit, all true. Achilles again wants to conclude *Z*. The Tortoise is again hesitant: just as before, the facts at hand aren't helpful unless we add an additional principle we'll call *D*:

> "*A*," "*A* entails *Z*," and "*C*" together entail "*Z*."

After granting this, Achilles then says that if you refuse to accept *Z* then "Logic would take you by the throat and force you to do it!" But sadly for Achilles (though happily for logicians) logic isn't the throat-grabbing sort and, as is clear, there's to be no end to the Tortoise's demands.

So much for the story. It's fun and interesting and has generated an enormous literature that we won't attempt to survey here – though I'll mention that a decent survey of the field can be found in §2.1 of Padro (2015). What I *do* want to do is point out that one natural interpretation of what's at issue between the Tortoise and Achilles draws on the distinction Slaney draws between using theories as guides to the facts and using theories as sources of inference tickets. More to the point, where Achilles seems to be using the entailments arrived at along the way as inference tickets, the Tortoise seems to be using them as no more than a guide to the facts. Neither one is wrong per se and to the extent that there's an error being made, it's the error of speaking past one another.

The point of all this – whether you prefer it Beall-flavored, Slaney-flavored, or Carroll-flavored – is that logic is intimately bound up with two distinct ways of combining theories. Here (for a variety of reasons) we're going to fudge the details a little bit: rather than a binary operation capturing the "combine *s* and *t* while taking *t* to be a guide to the facts" function, we'll instead provide a binary relation that plays the role of the "*s* is contained in *t*" relation. Given the usual sorts of interdefinability between relations of this sort and operations of the preceding sort, we don't take this to be a significant departure. And since it makes our lives much easier, we think it's warranted.[4]

---

[4] The reader who disagrees might want to have a look at Humberstone (1988), where they'll find the start of an examination of the matter from the other angle.

So (reviewing) the models we build will model spaces of theories. The things in our models that model theories will be connected to each other by a binary relation that models the containment relation that holds among theories and a binary operation that models what happens when we combine them in the second of the ways previously defined.

The next important observation is that we engage in a whole range of different theory-building *practices*, each giving rise to an entirely different space of theories. But theory-building practices aren't magic. They're describable. And the descriptions we give of the closure relations operative for a given theory-building practice are themselves (or are themselves flesh-out-able into) theories. And they are theories that play a particularly important role.

Since this is a point of departure from the story told in Beall (2017), Beall (2018), and Beall (2019), it's worth first reiterating where we *agree* with Beall's story. As with Beall, so also on the story told here theory building is essentially a matter of taking some sentences and fleshing them out. And I'm in agreement with Beall that it's important to note that in different settings and in the context of different goals, there are a range of ways one might do this. Where I diverge from Beall is in emphasizing the following fact: given a theory-building practice, we can characterize the practice by a set of entailments. And when we restrict our attention to *P-theories* – sets of sentences that (with respect to the theory-building practice *P*) are already fully fleshed-out – the set of entailments that characterizes *P* itself is algebraically distinguishable by the fact that it is a left identity for Achilles-wise combination. This for the simple reason that – now writing "$t \cdot u$" for the Achilles-wise combination of the theories t and u – if u is already a *P*-theory and t characterizes the entailments that flesh a set of sentences out into a *P*-theory, then $t \cdot u$ asks us to generate a *P*-theory using as data a set of sentences, u, that already counts as a *P*-theory. And we can do this. But the result is just u.

The picture then, is this: as we will model them, spaces of theories are endowed with a binary operation representing Achilles-wise/inference-ticket-wise combination of theories and a binary relation that does the work of Tortoise-wise/data-wise combination of theories. In addition, each space of theories is "pointed" in the sense that one of the theories in the space is distinguished as the theory-building theory at play in the space. For the reasons just discussed, this theory also serves as an identity for the Achilles-wise binary operation.

Not all structures with these features will model spaces of theories. Certain conditions will need to be imposed for the modeling to get off the ground. We'll have much more to say about this in the next section, but as an example, note that one thing we'll need to require is that the binary relation in play be a partial ordering. Otherwise, it can't do the work it needs to do vis-à-vis Tortoise-wise combination. But before going down this road any further, it's worthwhile to pause here to note something a bit magical that happens

The magic is this: all of the plausible candidate logics we can arrive at when pursuing this have certain formal properties that are naturally interpreted as meaning that they reject inferences in which the conclusion is irrelevant to the premise. Since arriving at logics that have this feature wasn't our *goal*, I think it's quite surprising that such logics are where we end up. But there's another way of looking at things on which it's not surprising at all. What we're looking for, after all, is the *minimal* relation that can plausibly be interpreted as a way of building theories. And while not all relations that meet this bar will preserve relevance, it seems that some will – after all, when I build theories in, say, biology, the result is seldom a theory that has anything at all to say about for example cosmology. So at least some of our theory-building practices – indeed, some of our most important examples of theory-building practices – look to be relevant. Thus we ought to expect the minimal such practice to be relevant.

Another, more explicable and less magical consequence of foregrounding theory-building is that the logics we build will be both paracomplete and paraconsistent. As a reminder, a logic is paracomplete when there are sentences A for which $A \lor \neg A$ is not validated and a logic is paraconsistent when there are sentences A and B for which $(A \land \neg A) \rightarrow B$ is not valid. That we end up paracomplete and paraconsistent is, I've said, not surprising. Here's why: Say what you will about whether inconsistent or incomplete theories are satisfying or plausible or what-have-you; it remains, in spite of whatever you've said, that inconsistent and incomplete theories are theories. And, having admitted inconsistent and incomplete theories, it'd be surprising if we *didn't* end up paracomplete and paraconsistent.

So there you have it. In the remainder of the Element, we'll spell out relevance logics from the theory-building perspective. It's an important perspective, and one whose roots go back to the very start of the field. But it's not the only perspective out there. In the final section of the Element, we'll talk a bit about other perspectives. The reader interested in learning more about these is invited to pick up any of the extant textbooks on relevance, since (to my knowledge at least) none of them cover it in the way I'm covering it here. Particularly helpful are Mares (2004) and Read (1988), which I'll also make mention of in what follows.

So much for the philosophical story. Let's actually get down to brass tacks and spell out our propositional semantics.

3 Propositional Models

The basic structure we will work in terms of is that of the *model*. As suggested earlier, what models *do*, at the end of the day, is model. And, as we've been banging on about, what they model are spaces of theories. Spaces of theories, in turn, are collections of theories with respect to some closure relation together with a natural family of operations hooking the theories up in various ways. We've said this much already. To say more, we have to start doing some math.

We will model spaces of *propositional* theories as 7-tuples. We'll label the positions in such a tuple, M, as follows:

$$\langle T_M, P_M, \sqsubseteq_M, \circ_M, \ell_M, \star_M, v_M \rangle.$$

That said, we'll seldom need to deploy the subscripts. We'll also occasionally want to say that a *frame* is the 6-tuple one gets from a model by leaving off its last component, v_M.

Qua model, here's how these tuples work. The elements of the initial triple $\langle T, P, \sqsubseteq \rangle$ model, respectively, the set of *T*heories being modeled, the distinguished subset of T containing the *P*rime theories, and the binary containment relation holding among the members of T. Intuitively, prime theories are the theories that contain at least one disjunct of each disjunction they contain. Or as said in Fine (1974), where these models were first introduced, the primes are the theories "that answer every either-or question they raise."

The next element, "$\circ$," is a binary operation on theories meant to model what we earlier called "Achilles-wise" combination. But rather than calling it this, we'll follow John Slaney's lead (see Slaney [1990]) and call it *application*. Intuitively, where t and u are theories, $t \circ u$ is the theory formed by discharging every inference ticket from t that one can while relying on the information in u. When we come to the completeness proof, this will be modeled by the function from pairs of sets of sentences to individual sets of sentences given by $\langle t, u \rangle \mapsto \{B : A \to B \in t \text{ and } A \in u\}$. Either way, it's the stuff you can infer from u using the rules in t.

Next up is ℓ. As a reminder from the discussion in the previous section, the thought to have regarding ℓ is this: what our models are models *of* is some space of theories for some closure relation or other. The closure relation, in turn, is a family of rules – a family of ways of saying when something belongs in the closure of (which is to say follows from) some set of formulas. In particular, for each formula A, the closure relation tells us that certain other formulas B follow from A. Taking all such pairs $\langle A, B \rangle$, we then form the set of all formulas $A \to B$ – the collection of all rules telling us that B follows from A, for each pair $\langle A, B \rangle$ for which B in fact follows from A according to the closure relation at hand. The theory generated by these formulas, ℓ, is the theory that describes the rules for closing a set of formulas under the closure relation at play in the space being modeled. In other words, it's the theory-building theory for the type of theory-building at hand. The observation to make (still repeating, though in a slightly different way, what was already said in the previous section) is the following: given any set t that already is a theory, if we apply ℓ to t, the result should be the theory generated by t. But since t already is a theory, t should itself be the theory generated by t. Thus $\ell \circ t$ should just be t, which is to say that ℓ is a left identity for $\circ$.

This leaves $\star$ and v unexplained. The second of these, v, records which atomic formulae are contained in which theories. The first is harder. In the literature, it is known as the Routley star. First introduced into relevance logics in Routley and Routley (1972), it nearly immediately generated controversy – see for example Copeland (1979). This controversy has, in turn, been revisited (and rerevisited!) numerous times – see Restall (1999) for a classic revisiting and Berto and Restall (2019) for a more recent revisiting.

Putting controversy aside for a moment, $\star$ is a unary operation on primes – a function from P to P. Intuitively, it models the function mapping each prime theory p to the theory generated by those formulas whose negations aren't contained in p. That this is a perfectly good function from sets of formulas to sets of formulas is clear enough. So the decision to include a model of such a function in our model of spaces of theories is, in principle at least, also ok. But one should wonder (a) whether it models anything familiar and (b) why on earth it's a thing worth worrying about.

Here's my take on the matter: in answer to question (a), I think the answer is "no." The Routley star is, at least from the perspective of modeling spaces of theories, something of a hack. But, now in answer to question (b), the point is that it's an effective hack. We'll see in what follows that with minimal assumptions, prime theories will turn out to be closed under the Routley star. And if we employ the Routley star, then we can use all the recursive tools of contemporary model theory to do neat things with a negation-including language. All told, since the star models a perfectly good function that there's no prohibition against modeling and since doing so lets us do cool things we couldn't do otherwise, it's worth getting used to it. But it's still a hack.[5]

---

[5] This is an at least mildly idiosyncratic take on the matter. There are other takes, including takes on which the Routley star is a Very Serious Thing Indeed. The papers mentioned above are a starting place for a discussion of the matter, and (as with most things we'll discuss) checking in on what Dunn had to say about the matter (by looking at e.g. Dunn (1993)) is never a bad idea.

Back to the thread: recall that our goal is to use 7-tuples composed of these elements as models of spaces of theories. Given this aim, there are natural restrictions that we should impose. Including the restrictions already identified, here are the requirements:

(1) $\emptyset \neq P$; $P \subseteq T$; and $\ell \in T$.

(2) $\sqsubseteq$ is a partial ordering of T.

(3) If $s \sqsubseteq t$ – that is, if s and t are taken to represent theories with s contained in t – then given any further theory u, we ought to have $u \circ s \sqsubseteq u \circ t$ and $s \circ u \sqsubseteq t \circ u$. After all, since t has at least as much in it as s does, applying anything to s should get us at least as much as we'd get by applying that same thing to t and applying s to anything should get us at least as much as we'd get if we applied t to that same thing.

(4) If $s \sqsubseteq t$, then, since s is supposed to represent a theory contained in the theory represented by t, the set of atoms in s, $v(s)$, should be contained in the set of atoms contained in t, $v(t)$. Succinctly, if $s \sqsubseteq t$, then $v(s) \subseteq v(t)$.

(5) $v(t)$ should be determined by the value of v at prime extensions of t. That is, if some atom a is contained in $v(p)$ for all primes $p \sqsupseteq t$, then a should be in t as well. Succinctly, $\bigcap_{t \sqsubseteq p \in P} v(p) \subseteq v(t)$. Boiling down to the simplest case, the idea here is this: if some disjunction $B_1 \vee B_2$ is in t and both disjuncts B_i force us to accept some atom a, then t itself is already committed to – and thus must include – a. So we can figure out what atoms have to be in t by just looking at those atoms that are in all of t's prime extensions.

(6) $\circ$ is also bounded by primes: if $t \circ u \sqsubseteq p \in P$, then there are $t \sqsubseteq q \in P$ and $u \sqsubseteq r \in P$ so that $q \circ u \sqsubseteq p$ and $t \circ r \sqsubseteq p$. Intuitively, this condition requires there to be enough primes and for the primes to be sufficiently densely distributed. What the condition explicitly requires is this: suppose we apply t to u, then settle all the either-or sentences that arise. Then we won't have missed anything that we could have gotten by first settling the either-or sentences in t or first settling the either-or sentences in u.

(7) $\star$ is an involution: there are two parts to the explanation of this. One part just concerns facts about containment. The other reflects an assumption we're making about the behavior of negation. Anyways, note that intuitively, A is in $p^{\star\star}$ just if $\neg A$ isn't in $p^{\star}$ just if $\neg\neg A$ is in p. This much just concerns containment. If we now suppose that $\neg\neg A$ entails A, we get what we need, namely that $p^{\star\star} = p$.[6]

---

[6] You might have come to this footnote wondering what things would be like if we didn't make this assumption. For the start of an answer, there's no better place to look than Robles and Méndez (2018) to which I defer so completely that we'll in fact not mention the matter again in this Element.

(8) ⋆ flips containment: if $p \sqsubseteq q$, then $q^\star \sqsubseteq p^\star$. This follows immediately
from the fact that if p is contained in q then things not contained in q aren't
contained in p.

As the descriptions of the preceding conditions hopefully make clear, this turns
the 7-tuples described previously into actual models of spaces of theories.

Our goal, we remind you, is to find the minimal theory-building theory. It's
now clear what this requires: since A is intuitively in ℓ_M just if A is part of the
theory-building theory at play in the space of theories modeled by M, A is in
the minimal theory-building theory just if A is in ℓ_M for all M.

To say more about this, we need to give a recursive procedure for determining
when A is in a given theory t. But we should note that in general, nothing in
the definition requires the points in a model to be sets. So the relation we'll
recursively define is not literally set-containment. Rather, it's a relation that's
meant to *model* containment. So we'll follow Fine in calling the relation we
define *commitment*. For a given sentence A, theory t, and model M, we write
"$M, t \vDash A$" to mean that in M, t is committed to A.

Before we go any further at all, though, we need to define our language.

Definition 3.1 *Let* At $= \{p_i\}_{i=1}^{\infty}$ *be a set of atomic formulas. Then we define
the basic propositional language* $\mathcal{L}^p$ *by saying that every member of* At *is a
sentence and that whenever X and Y are sentences of* $\mathcal{L}^p$, *so are* $\neg X$, $(X \wedge Y)$,
$(X \vee Y)$, *and* $(X \to Y)$.

From time to time, we'll also make use of the biconditional "$\leftrightarrow$", which we
take be a defined connective in the usual way; viz. $A \leftrightarrow B =_{def} (A \to B) \wedge
(B \to A)$.

We now define $\vDash$ as follows:

- For $a \in$ At, $t \vDash a$ iff $a \in v(t)$.
- $t \vDash \neg A$ iff $p^\star \nvDash A$ for all $t \sqsubseteq p \in P$.
- $t \vDash A \wedge B$ iff $t \vDash A$ and $t \vDash B$.
- $t \vDash A \vee B$ iff for all $t \sqsubseteq p \in P$ either $p \vDash A$ or $p \vDash B$.
- $t \vDash A \to B$ iff for all u, if $u \vDash A$, then $t \circ u \vDash B$.

Bearing in mind that commitment is meant to model containment, we can
justify these clauses as follows:

- The atomic clause is justified by the explanation already provided for v.
- The negation clause is justified by (a) the intuition that primes should be
  determinative not just for atoms, but generally (though this is an intuition

we'll have to back up in the discussion that follows) and (b) the explanation already provided for $\star$.

- The conjunction clause can really only be explained by appeal to the brute intuition that no set containing A and B and not containing $A \wedge B$ can possibly count as "sufficiently fleshed out."
- The disjunction clause is immediate from our understanding of primality.
- Finally, for entailments note that, if t is committed to $A \rightarrow B$, then given the explanations we've already provided for the "$\circ$" operation, it must be the case that if u is committed to A then $t \circ u$ is committed to B. For the other direction, we suggest that the reader have a look at the completeness proof – see in particular the proof of Lemma 4.31.

And now we can at last finish the job: for a model M, say that M verifies A (and write $M \vDash A$) when $\ell_M \vDash A$. Say that A is valid (and write $\vDash A$) when $M \vDash A$ for all models M. The thing we are after – the minimal theory-building theory – is the set of all such A.

3.1 Important Results

It's not completely obvious that we've actually done our job. That is, it's not obvious that we've put sufficient conditions in place to ensure that the models behave like they ought. Here, in particular, are three reasonable worries:

Worry 1: Do the models track containment appropriately? That is, if $s \sqsubseteq t$ and $s \vDash A$, does it follow that $t \vDash A$? Since "$\sqsubseteq$" is supposed to model containment and $\vDash$ is supposed to model elementhood, this had better be the case. But as it stands, we've only demanded that this condition be met at the atomic level.

Worry 2: Are the primes determinative everywhere? That is, if $p \vDash A$ for all $t \sqsubseteq p \in P$, does it follow that $t \vDash A$? One expects this to be the case – if $p \vDash A$ for all $t \sqsubseteq p \in P$, then no matter how we settle the disjunctions in t, we end up committed to A. Exactly as previously, this again suggests that t ought to contain A – which is to say that we ought to have $t \vDash A$.

Worry 3: Does the star operation in fact give rise to the appropriate sort of duality? That is, do we have that $p^\star \vDash A$ just if $p \nvDash \neg A$? Again, given what everything in sight is meant to model, this had better be the case.

We end this section by stating without proof a few results that tell us that we can rest easy on these fronts:

Theorem 3.2 *If $s \sqsubseteq t$ and $s \vDash A$, then $t \vDash A$ as well.*

Theorem 3.3 *If $p \vDash A$ for all $t \sqsubseteq p \in P$, then $t \vDash A$ as well.*

Theorem 3.4 *For all $p \in P$, $p^\star \vDash A$ just if $p \nvDash \neg A$.*

Finally, we note that it really is the case that every theory is closed under the rules in the logic in the sense that

Theorem 3.5 *$\ell \vDash A \to B$ if and only if for all t if $t \vDash A$, then $t \vDash B$.*

3.2 Concluding Thoughts

Before moving in, let's recall what we've accomplished so far. The goal was to model spaces of theories. We've modeled them as models which, in turn, are 7-tuples of a certain sort. We've seen that models have features that make it plausible they do in fact model spaces of theories. And we've seen that there is a way of defining, with respect to the class of models, a set of formulas that really is the universal theory-building theory. What we'll turn to next is determining the contents of the universal theory-building theory by directly axiomatizing it.

4 Axiomatizing the Propositional Logic

The set of validities of the semantic theory given in the previous section goes by the rather inauspicious name "**B**". Note the boldface here – throughout the remainder of the Element, we will reserve boldface letters as names of logics.

While there are weaker logics that sometimes fall under the relevant umbrella – some of which are mentioned in the final section of the Element – **B** is nonetheless typically taken to be something like "the most basic" relevant logic. It is, in any event, the logic we'll spend most of our time examining.

Axiomatically, we can characterize **B** as follows:

A1. $A \to A$

A2. $(A \land B) \to A$; $(A \land B) \to B$

A3. $((A \to B) \land (A \to C)) \to (A \to (B \land C))$

A4. $A \to (A \lor B)$; $B \to (A \lor B)$

A5. $((A \to C) \land (B \to C)) \to ((A \lor B) \to C)$

A6. $(A \land (B \lor C)) \to ((A \land B) \lor (A \land C))$

A7. $\neg\neg A \to A$

R1. $\dfrac{A \qquad A \to B}{B}$

R2. $\dfrac{A \qquad B}{A \land B}$

R3. $\dfrac{A \to B \qquad C \to D}{(B \to C) \to (A \to D)}$

R4. $\dfrac{A \to \neg B}{B \to \neg A}$

Being explicit, we can define **B** to be the set of all formulas A for which there is a sequence $A_1, \ldots, A_n$ with $A_n = A$ so that for $1 \le i \le n$, either

- A_i is an instance of one of A1–A7 or
- There are $j < i$ and $k < i$ so that $A_k = A_j \to A_i$ or
- There are $j < i$ and $k < i$ so that $A_i = A_j \wedge A_k$ or
- There are $j < i$ and $k < i$ so that $A_j = A_j^1 \to A_j^2$ and $A_k = A_k^1 \to A_k^2$ and $A_i = (A_j^2 \to A_k^1) \to (A_j^1 \to A_k^2)$.
- There is $j < i$ so that $A_j = A_j^1 \to \neg A_j^2$ and $A_i = A_j^2 \to \neg A_j^1$.

We call a sequence of A_i's meeting these conditions a *derivation* of A and we call the derivable things (which is to say the members of **B**) *theorems* of **B**. Here are a few things we can say about what's in **B** that we'll have need of in what follows:

Lemma 4.1 *Each of the following is a theorem-scheme of* **B**:

- $(A \to B) \to (A \to (B \vee C))$
- $(A \to B) \to ((A \wedge C) \to B)$
- $((A \wedge B) \vee C) \to ((A \vee C) \wedge (B \vee C))$
- $\neg(A \vee B) \leftrightarrow (\neg A \wedge \neg B)$
- $\neg(A \wedge B) \leftrightarrow (\neg A \vee \neg B)$

Lemma 4.2 *If* $(A_1 \wedge B_1) \to C_1 \in \mathbf{B}$ *and* $(A_2 \wedge B_2) \to C_2 \in \mathbf{B}$, *then* $((A_1 \wedge A_2) \wedge (B_1 \vee B_2)) \to (C_1 \vee C_2) \in \mathbf{B}$.

Lemma 4.3 *If* $A \to A' \in \mathbf{B}$, *then for all B,* $(A' \to B) \to (A \to B) \in \mathbf{B}$.

Lemma 4.4 (Transitivity for B) *If* $A \to B \in \mathbf{B}$ *and* $B \to C \in \mathbf{B}$, *then* $A \to C \in \mathbf{B}$.

Relevance logics are often better characterized, though, in terms of what they *don't* prove than in terms of what they *do*. So we'll turn in a moment to stating some things one *can't* prove in **B**. Before doing so, we'll discuss the most useful tool we have for demonstrating unprovability: John Slaney's Matrix Generator for Implication Connectives – also known as MaGIC.[7]

For serious work in relevance logics, MaGIC is indispensable. It is freely and easily found, as of this writing, on John Slaney's personal website. Since MaGIC *is* so indispensable, it's worth our while to briefly discuss both how

---

[7] For a detailed description of MaGIC's inner workings, see Slaney (1995).

```
Logic:          B

Fragment:       ->, &, v, ~, t, f, T, F

TTY output:     pretty
File output:    none

Search concludes when size 14 finished.


    A)xiom     B)adguy      C)onnective    D)elete
    E)xit      F)ragment    G)enerate      H)elp
    I)O        J)ump        K)ill          L)ogic
    M)aGIC     N)o. Procs   O)rder         P)rint Opts
    Q)uit      R)ead        S)tore
```

Figure 1 MaGIC, just after you've chosen to work in **B**

```
Shall I stop when: (a) I'm exhausted?
                   (b) time's up?
                   (c) I've found enough matrices?
                   (d) the matrices get too big?
                   (e) a combination of the above?
```

Figure 2 MaGIC asking when to stop

to use it and how to understand the information MaGIC provides. On the first front, we'll simply assume that the reader is capable of finding, installing, and starting up MaGIC. When one does so, the first question MaGIC asks is what your favorite logic is. Since our focus here is on **B**, respond with "B". At this point, the reader should see something that looks roughly like Figure 1.

Most of the options presented at the bottom are either self-explanatory or are well explained in the documentation that comes with MaGIC. For our purposes, the important options are Axiom, Badguy, Generate, Jump, and Logic. Logic, as is probably expected, is used to change what logic one is using. Axiom, on the other hand, allows one to add additional axioms, which is helpful when working with logics that MaGIC doesn't already have built in.

Of the other three, Generate is essentially a "start" command while Jump is the option you choose in order to tell MaGIC what sort of work you're looking to have it do. If we choose this option, MaGIC asks us (as seen in Figure 2) when it should "stop."

In order to answer this question, we first need to know a little bit about what MaGIC is going to do for us. The long and the short of it is that – while it can do other things – we'll be using MaGIC to generate a certain sort of counterexample to a sentence we provide it. Depending on your purposes, then, you can decide what sort of search MaGIC should perform in looking for this counterexample. If (as is often the case) all you want to know is whether something is a theorem, then one counterexample will suffice. So you should tell MaGIC

```
Shall I stop when: (a) I'm exhausted?
                   (b) time's up?
                   (c) I've found enough matrices?
                   (d) the matrices get too big?
                   (e) a combination of the above?        e

How many matrices are enough?  1

How big can they get?          0

How many seconds have I got?   100
```

Figure 3 Telling MaGIC when to stop

to stop when it has found enough counterexamples (option (c)) and then tell it that one matrix (counterexample) is enough.

The problem is that MaGIC might search and search for a counterexample and never find one. So you might also want to tell it to stop when it's looked for long enough (that is, until time's up; option (b)) or when it's looked through big-enough counterexamples (option (d)). Otherwise, you can tell it to run until it's 'exhausted' (option (a)), in which case it will run for a very long time.

Of course, one can have other intentions in mind. Maybe, for example, one wants to know what counterexamples to a given sentence look like in general (so that multiple counterexamples might be helpful). In that case, you might tell it you want some number of counterexamples larger than one, and either give it a time limit or not. And so on – you get the point.

Let's suppose for now that what we really want to know is whether *there is* a counterexample to some formula, and that we're willing to wait no more than 100 seconds to find out. Then we choose option (e), since we want a combination of the options MaGIC has provided. It then asks us how many matrices are enough (we say "1" because we just want to know if there is a counterexample), then how big they can get (we say "0" because we don't care) and then how many seconds we'll give it (100). If you stop here (before pressing return) you should see essentially what's in Figure 3. Pressing return then brings us back to the starting point, but with the new settings recorded, as in Figure 4.

The final thing to do before actually *using* MaGIC is to tell it what we want it to look for a counterexample *to*. Let's start with something that doesn't take too long to run: $A \rightarrow (B \rightarrow (A \wedge B))$. To ask MaGIC to find counterexamples to this, you set it as the Badguy by first entering "B", then typing in the formula as seen in Figure 5.

After pressing return, you can then ask MaGIC to Generate. The result (which should come quickly) should look roughly like what's in Figure 6.

As seen in in Figure 6, MaGIC actually gives us quite a bit of information. What this information *does* is give us a way to prove that $A \rightarrow (B \rightarrow (A \wedge B))$

```
Logic:          B

Fragment:       ->, &, v, ~, t, f, T, F

TTY output:     pretty
File output:    none

Search concludes after 100 seconds
or when 1 matrix found
or when size 14 finished.


    A)xiom      B)adguy     C)onnective   D)elete
    E)xit       F)ragment   G)enerate     H)elp
    I)O         J)ump       K)ill         L)ogic
    M)aGIC      N)o. Procs  O)rder        P)rint Opts
    Q)uit       R)ead       S)tore                      ▯
```

Figure 4 Back to the starting point

```
Logic:          B

Fragment:       ->, &, v, ~, t, f, T, F

TTY output:     pretty
File output:    none

Search concludes after 100 seconds
or when 1 matrix found
or when size 14 finished.


    A)xiom      B)adguy     C)onnective   D)elete
    E)xit       F)ragment   G)enerate     H)elp
    I)O         J)ump       K)ill         L)ogic
    M)aGIC      N)o. Procs  O)rder        P)rint Opts
    Q)uit       R)ead       S)tore

                                                     B


Enter formula (or RETURN):  A->(B->(A&B))▯
```

Figure 5 Declaring the Badguy

is *not* a theorem of **B**. It does this by providing, in the line "Failure: 2 -> (0 -> (2 & 0))", a particular counterexample: the counterexample where *A* is mapped to 2 and *B* is mapped to 0. What's crucial to understand is that this is not a counterexample in the semantics we've been examining. Instead it's a counterexample in a sound-but-incomplete semantics that's entirely specified by the text MaGIC has provided.

Here's how to read that information off of what MaGIC has provided. First, the middle piece of information – the table under "Order 3.1.1", tells us we will be interpreting the language in a three-valued model containing the elements 0, 1, and 2, ordered so that $0 \leq 1 \leq 2$. MaGIC also tells you what

```
            Size: 3

            Negation table 3.1

                  a | 0 1 2
                 ---+------
                 ~a | 2 1 0


            Order 3.1.1

                  < | 0 1 2
                 --+------
                  0 | + + +
                  1 | - + +
                  2 | - - +


            Choice 3.1.1.1 of t:  1


            Implication matrix 3.1.1.1.1

                 -> | 0 1 2
                 ---+------
                  0 | 1 1 1
                  1 | 0 1 1
                  2 | 0 0 1

            Failure: 2 -> (0 -> (2 & 0))
```

Figure 6 MaGICal Results!

the "designated values" are by telling you that the Choice...*of t* is 1. This means that 1 and everything "above" 1 in the ordering it gives counts as a way of being true. MaGIC *does* tell you how ¬ and → are to be interpreted via the "negation table" and "implication matrix"; more on this in a moment. It *doesn't* tell you how ∧ and ∨ are to be interpreted, because they're always interpreted as min and max, respectively.

There's an implicit claim being made in the information MaGIC is present-ing that's worth spelling out. Say that a valuation is a function from atomic formulas to $\{0, 1, 2\}$. Let $M_\neg$ be the (unary) function given by the negation table MaGIC provided and $M_\rightarrow$ be the (binary) function given by the implica-tion matrix MaGIC provided. Now given a valuation v, extend v to a function on our entire language by the following recursive clauses:

1. $v(\neg A) = M_\neg(v(A))$.
2. $v(A \wedge B) = \min(v(A), v(B))$.
3. $v(A \vee B) = \max(v(A), v(B))$.
4. $v(A \rightarrow B) = M_\rightarrow(v(A), v(B))$.

Here in clauses (2) and (3), we take the minimums and maximums to be with respect to the ordering MaGIC specified.

The claim that MaGIC is then implicitly making is this: If $A \in \mathbf{B}$, then $v(A)$ is designated for all valuations v. The reader who thinks they're likely to make use of MaGIC in the future is encouraged to pause at this point to prove (probably by induction on derivations) that this is actually a *true* claim.

Either way, the point is that MaGIC told us all of *that* so that it could tell us how to see that $A \to (B \to (A \wedge B))$ *is not* a theorem of $\mathbf{B}$: simply assign A to 2 and B to 0, and we assign $A \to (B \to (A \wedge B))$ to a nondesignated value; namely 0, as we recommend that the reader check. Since valuations in the preceding sense always *do* assign all theorems to a designated value but the particular valuation described *doesn't* assign $A \to (B \to (A \wedge B))$ to a designated value, it follows that $A \to (B \to (A \wedge B))$ must not be a theorem of $\mathbf{B}$.

Hopefully this makes clear that MaGIC (a) is an incredibly useful resource and (b) carries quite a bit of information in a very small package. Periodically throughout the Element, we will use MaGIC to say when this or that is a non-theorem. When we do so, the reader is invited to fire up their own copy of MaGIC and check for themselves. Finally, because it's crucial to understand, I will emphasize again that the matrix-valued semantic theories that MaGIC provides give us sound but (typically very) incomplete semantic theories. As an example, it's not too hard to see that valuations in the three-valued matrix given earlier always assign $(A \wedge (A \to B)) \to B$ a designated value. But as MaGIC itself is happy to tell us (go check!) this is a nontheorem of $\mathbf{B}$.

In any event, as mentioned already, you're likely to get a better feel for $\mathbf{B}$ by thinking about what *isn't* a theorem than by thinking about what *is*. To that end, here are some additional nontheorems. We leave the (MaGICal or otherwise) verification of their nontheoremhood to the reader:

- $A \to (B \to A)$
- $A \to ((A \to B) \to B)$
- $(A \to (A \to B)) \to (A \to B)$
- $(A \to B) \to (A \to (A \to B))$
- $(A \to \neg B) \to (B \to \neg A)$
- $((A \to B) \wedge (B \to C)) \to (A \to C)$
- $(A \to \neg A) \to \neg A$
- $(A \to B) \to ((B \to C) \to (A \to C))$
- $(A \to B) \to ((C \to A) \to (C \to B))$
- $A \vee \neg A$

4.1 Metatheory

We'll now turn to showing that the axiomatization we gave of $\mathbf{B}$ is in fact correct. We don't do this solely for the sake of rigor. We also do it because our understanding of $\mathbf{B}$ as the universal theory-building theory lends a special importance to the metatheory, and in particular to the completeness proof.

Theorem 4.5 (Soundness) *If A is a theorem of **B**, then A is valid.*

Proof: By induction on the length of the derivation of A. For the base case of our induction we need to demonstrate that every instance of every axiom is valid. I'll prove this for A3 and leave the rest of the cases to the reader.

For A3: By Theorem 3.5, $((A \to B) \wedge (A \to C)) \to (A \to (B \wedge C))$ is valid if and only if $t \vDash (A \to B) \wedge (A \to C)$, then $t \vDash A \to (B \wedge C)$ for all models M and all $t \in M$. So, suppose that $t \vDash (A \to B) \wedge (A \to C)$. Then $t \vDash A \to B$ and $t \vDash A \to C$. To see that $t \vDash A \to (B \wedge C)$, we suppose $u \vDash A$ and show that $t \circ u \vDash B \wedge C$ as follows. Since $t \vDash A \to B$, $t \circ u \vDash B$. And since $t \vDash A \to C$, $t \circ u \vDash C$. Thus $t \circ u \vDash B$ and $t \circ u \vDash C$. So $t \circ u \vDash B \wedge C$.

Base case completed we turn to our rules, each of which must be considered separately. I will give the argument for the R3 case and leave the rest to the reader. So, suppose $A \to B$ and $C \to D$ are both valid. By Theorem 3.5, $(B \to C) \to (A \to D)$ is valid just if for all models M and all $t \in M$, if $t \vDash B \to C$, then $t \vDash A \to D$. So suppose $t \vDash B \to C$. To see that $t \vDash A \to D$, we suppose $u \vDash A$ and show $t \circ u \vDash D$ as follows. Since $A \to B$ is valid, $\ell_M \vDash A \to B$. Thus $\ell_M \circ u = u \vDash B$. So since $t \vDash B \to C$, $t \circ u \vDash C$. Finally, since $C \to D$ is valid, $\ell_M \vDash C \to D$. But then $\ell_M \circ (t \circ u) = t \circ u \vDash D$. ■

We now turn to completeness. The basic idea of our completeness proof is to actually construct a space of theories for which **B** is the theory-building theory and to then demonstrate that this space falsifies every nontheorem. Since this demonstrates that all nontheorems are falsifiable, it suffices to show that not only all but also only theorems are valid. But note that it also demonstrates – and demonstrates quite concretely – that in at least one case, our intuitions about the structure of the space of theories are dead on. Thus, rather than being an ad hoc construction, the canonical model is, in some sense, "the intended model" of the logic. In any event, the first thing we need is to marshal an army of definitions.

Definition 4.6 *Say that B follows from Γ – and write $\Gamma \vdash B$ – just if there is a sequence $A_1, A_2, \ldots, A_n = B$ so that for all i, either*

(a) $A_i \in \Gamma$ or
(b) there are $j < i$ and $k < i$ so that $A_i = A_j \wedge A_k$ or
(c) for some $j < i$, $A_j \to A_i \in \textbf{B}$.

Any such sequence is called a derivation of B from Γ.

Definition 4.7 *We say that Γ is a formal theory when $\Gamma \vdash B$ just if $B \in \Gamma$. We write* Th *for the set of all formal theories.*

Definition 4.8 *The* formal theory generated by *s*, $\|s\|$, *is* $\{B : s \vdash B\}$.

Definition 4.9 *We say that a set of sentences is* closed under disjunction *when it contains $A \vee B$ whenever it contains both A and B.*

Definition 4.10 *A formal theory is* prime *when it contains at least one disjunct of each disjunction it contains;* Pr *is the set of all prime formal theories.*

Definition 4.11 *Formal application is the binary operation defined by* $t \cdot u = \{B : A \rightarrow B \in t$ and $A \in u\}$.

Definition 4.12 *The* formal dual, s^*, *of a set of sentences s is* $\{B : \neg B \notin s\}$.

To get a handle on these concepts, it helps to use them to prove a few things we'll need to use later anyways. We'll provide one of the proofs to help get things moving and leave the rest to the reader.

Lemma 4.13 *If* $B \in \|A_1\|$ *and* $B \in \|A_2\|$, *then* $B \in \|A_1 \vee A_2\|$.

Lemma 4.14 *t is a formal theory iff* $t = \|t\|$.

Lemma 4.15 *If* $\{A\} \vdash B$, *then* $A \rightarrow B \in \mathbf{B}$.

Proof: By induction on the derivation of *B* from $\{A\}$. If the derivation has length 1, then $A = B$, and since $A \rightarrow A \in \mathbf{B}$, we are done. Now suppose we have the result for derivations of length at most *n* and we have on hand a derivation of length $n+1$. If the last step was (a) from Definition 4.6 then again $B = A$ and we are done. If the last step was (b), then there are A_j and A_i with $j \leq n$ and $i \leq n$ so that $B = A_i \wedge A_j$. By the inductive hypothesis, $A \rightarrow A_i \in \mathbf{B}$ and $A \rightarrow A_j \in \mathbf{B}$. Thus by R1 and an instance of A3, $A \rightarrow (A_i \wedge A_j) = A \rightarrow B \in \mathbf{B}$ as required. If the last step was (c), then there is A_i with $i \leq n$ so that $A_i \rightarrow B \in \mathbf{B}$. But then by the inductive hypothesis, $A \rightarrow A_i \in \mathbf{B}$ as well. So by R3, an instance of A1, and R1, $A \rightarrow B \in \mathbf{B}$ as required. ∎

Corollary 4.16 *If* $\{A, B\} \vdash C$, *then* $(A \wedge B) \rightarrow C \in \mathbf{B}$.

Definitions in place, the canonical model is the following 7-tuple:

$$\langle \mathsf{Th}, \mathsf{Pr}, \mathbf{B}, \cdot, *, \subseteq, - \cap \mathsf{At} \rangle$$

The seventh spot here – the spot occupied by "$-\cap\mathsf{At}$" – means that the valuation is the function given by $t \mapsto t \cap \mathsf{At}$. This is called *the canonical valuation.*

The reader should note that the canonical model is exactly what it *should* be – its theories are the formal theories; its primes the prime formal theories; its logic is the logic; and so on. Even so, we still need to check that it *really is* a model. Before doing *that*, though, we need the following results:

Lemma 4.17 *B is a formal theory.*

Lemma 4.18 *If s and t are formal theories, so is s · t.*

Lemma 4.19 *If p is a prime formal theory, then so is p^*.*

Proof: One can show that p^* is a formal theory by induction on derivations. To see that p^* is prime, suppose $A \notin p^*$ and $B \notin p^*$. Then $\neg A \in p$ and $\neg B \in p$. So $\neg A \wedge \neg B \in p$. By Lemma 4.1, $(\neg A \wedge \neg B) \rightarrow \neg(A \vee B) \in \mathbf{B}$. So $\neg(A \vee B) \in p$ and thus $A \vee B \notin p^*$. So p^* is prime. ∎

Looking ahead, there are two things left to do in our completeness proof. First, we need to check that the canonical model is in fact a model; second, we need to check that commitment and containment match up – that is that $t \vDash A$ if and only if $A \in t$. Each of these tasks will end up being broken into several smaller parts, so it'll look as if we're doing a lot more than this. But really we aren't.

Turning first to the matter of modelhood, note that the canonical model satisfies (1)–(4) essentially by definition. (5)–(6), on the other hand, require a very important tool:

Lemma 4.20 (Lindenbaum) *Suppose that t is a formal theory, Δ is a set of formulas that is closed under disjunction, and $t \cap \Delta = \emptyset$. Then there is a prime formal theory $p \supseteq t$ so that $p \cap \Delta = \emptyset$.*

For a given t and Δ we will call the p that the lemma gives us "the extension of t away from Δ". The proof of Lemma 4.20 is, unfortunately, too long to include in its entirety. So we give only the general idea of the proof.

Proof Sketch: Choose an enumeration $L_0 \vee R_0, L_1 \vee R_1, \ldots$ of all the disjunctions in our language. For $0 \leq i < \infty$ and $0 \leq j < \infty$, define t_j^i as follows:

- $t_0^0 = t$

- $t_{j+1}^i = t_j^i$ if $L_j \vee R_j \notin \|t_j^i\|$

- Otherwise, $t_{j+1}^i = \begin{cases} t_j^i \cup \{L_j\} & \text{if } \|t_j^i \cup \{L_j\}\| \cap \Delta = \emptyset \\ t_j^i \cup \{R_j\} & \text{otherwise} \end{cases}$

- $t_0^{i+1} = \bigcup_{j=0}^{\infty} t_j^i$.

Then it turns out that $p = \bigcup_{i=0}^{\infty} t_0^i$ is a prime formal theory that contains t without intersecting Δ, as required. Some notes: intuitively, what we've done is this: at each stage in the construction, the first thing we check is whether we can prove the disjunction we're looking at. If we can, then if the left disjunct is "safe" to add, we add it. Otherwise, we add the right disjunct. We do this while going through all the disjunctions in the language. Along the way we may end up adding new disjunctions. So we have to go through again. And then again. But intuitively at each stage, we're adding less and less complex disjunctions. So after we go through all the disjunctions infinitely many times, we should be done. In any event, the hard part of the proof is showing that p doesn't intersect Δ. This is typically done by supposing p *does* intersect Δ, then looking at the first set t_j^i for which $\|t_j^i\|$ meets Δ. By carefully keeping track of the information this gives you, you'll see that in fact $\|t_{j-1}^i\|$ must also meet Δ, which is a contradiction.   ∎

We can put the Lindenbaum Lemma through its paces by looking at the proofs of a few lemmas:

Lemma 4.21 *If t and u are formal theories and $t \cdot u \subseteq p \in \mathrm{Pr}$, then there is $t \subseteq q \in \mathrm{Pr}$ so that $q \cdot u \subseteq p$.*

Proof Sketch: Let Δ be the set of all the things that'll get you in trouble, then show that Δ is closed under disjunction and use the Lindenbaum Lemma to extend t away from Δ. In more detail, let $\Delta = \{A : \|A\| \cdot u \not\subseteq p\}$. Each member of Δ is something that "gets us in trouble" in the sense of forcing us out of p. Since it's clear that $t \cap \Delta = \emptyset$ to finish the proof, one need only show that Δ is closed under disjunction, then let the Lindenbaum Lemma do its thing.   ∎

Lemma 4.22 *If t is a formal theory, then $t = \bigcap_{t \subseteq p \in \mathrm{Pr}} p$.*

Proof: That $t \subseteq \bigcap_{t \subseteq p \in \mathrm{Pr}} p$ is clear. Now suppose that $A \notin t$. Let Δ be the disjunctive closure of A – that is, the smallest set containing A and also containing disjunctions of any formulas it contains. Since $A \notin t$, $t \cap \Delta = \emptyset$. By the Lindenbaum Lemma, it follows that there is a prime that extends t away from Δ. Since this prime extension thus doesn't contain A, it follows that $\bigcap_{t \subseteq p \in \mathrm{Pr}} p$ also doesn't contain A.   ∎

Lemma 4.23 $\emptyset \neq \mathrm{Pr};$ $\mathrm{Pr} \subseteq \mathrm{Th};$ *and* $\mathbf{B} \in \mathrm{Th}$.

Proof: Only the first requires explanation. In the previous section, we saw that there are things that aren't in $\mathbf{B}$. Choose one of them and let Δ be its disjunctive closure. Then $\mathbf{B} \cap \Delta = \emptyset$. So by the Lindenbaum Lemma there is a prime that extends $\mathbf{B}$ away from Δ. Thus, in particular, there is a prime. ∎

Now we're finally in position to show that the canonical model is in fact a model. There are seven conditions to check, covered by the following lemmas:

Lemma 4.24 $\subseteq$ *is a partial ordering of* Th.

Lemma 4.25 *If* $s \subseteq t$, *then* $u \cdot s \subseteq u \cdot t$ *and* $s \cdot u \subseteq t \cdot u$.

Lemma 4.26 *If* $s \subseteq t$, *then* $s \cap$ At $\subseteq t \cap$ At.

Lemma 4.27 $\bigcap_{t \subseteq p \in \Pr} v(p) \subseteq v(t)$.

Lemma 4.28 *If* $t \cdot u \subseteq p \in \Pr$, *then there are* $t \subseteq q \in \Pr$ *and* $u \subseteq r \in \Pr$ *so that* $q \cdot u \subseteq p$ *and* $t \cdot r \subseteq p$.

Proof Sketch: One half of this is Lemma 4.21. As a hint for the other half, let $\Delta = \{A : t \cdot \|A\| \nsubseteq p\}$. ∎

Lemma 4.29 $p^{**} = p$.

Lemma 4.30 *If* $p \subseteq q$, *then* $q^* \subseteq p^*$.

This leaves us with only one thing left to check:

Lemma 4.31 *In the canonical model,* $t \vDash A$ *if and only if* $A \in t$.

Proof: By induction on the complexity of A. I present the trickier direction of the conditional case and leave the remainder to the reader.

Suppose $A \to B \notin t$. I claim that $B \notin t \cdot \|A\|$. Note that by the inductive hypothesis, it follows that $t \nvDash A \to B$. To see that $B \notin t \cdot \|A\|$, suppose to the contrary. Then there is $A' \in \|A\|$ with $A' \to B \in t$. But since $A' \in \|A\|$, it follows by Lemma 4.15 that $A \to A' \in \mathbf{B}$. But then by Lemma 4.3, $(A' \to B) \to (A \to B) \in \mathbf{B}$ as well. So since $A' \to B \in t$, $A \to B \in t$, which is a contradiction. ∎

Theorem 4.32 *If* A *is valid, then* A *is a theorem of* $\mathbf{B}$.

Proof: We prove the contrapositive. Suppose A is not a theorem of $\mathbf{B}$. Then by Lemma 4.31, $\mathbf{B}$ in the cannonical model does not verify A. So A is not verified in every model, and is thus invalid. ∎

4.2 Extensions of B

Here we briefly discuss a few of the more popular extensions of **B** that can be found in the literature and we describe how we have to change our models to capture them. Readers who want a more exhaustive characterization than the one we give will be able to find many options in the literature – though the chart in Brady (1984b) is often particularly useful. The logics we describe are all extensions of **B**. Each strengthens **B** by adding some of the following axioms:

Contraposition $(A \rightarrow \neg B) \rightarrow (B \rightarrow \neg A)$
Suffixing $(A \rightarrow B) \rightarrow ((B \rightarrow C) \rightarrow (A \rightarrow C))$
Prefixing $(A \rightarrow B) \rightarrow ((C \rightarrow A) \rightarrow (C \rightarrow B))$
Contraction $(A \rightarrow (A \rightarrow B)) \rightarrow (A \rightarrow B)$
Commutativity $A \rightarrow ((A \rightarrow B) \rightarrow B)$

As we've already MaGICally verified, none of these is a theorem of **B**. So adding any of them to **B** results in a genuine extension. Many of these extensions have names, but we'll focus for now on just the following systems:

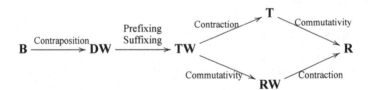

These five extensions of **B** are by no means the only extensions that have been studied. Nor do they even exhaust the most extensively studied such extensions, such as the logic **E** was the target of much of the discussion in Anderson and Belnap (1975) and (to a lesser extent) in Anderson et al. (1992). But they do make a tidy package of logics to look at, so it's where we'll stop.

Semantically, we model the preceding logics by restricting to classes of models that satisfy certain conditions. The restrictions in question are the following:

To model logics with . . .	Restrict to models satisfying . . .
Contraposition	if $t \circ p \sqsubseteq q$, then $t \circ q^\star \sqsubseteq p^\star$.
Suffixing	$t \circ (u \circ v) \sqsubseteq (u \circ t) \circ v$
Prefixing	$t \circ (u \circ v) \sqsubseteq (t \circ u) \circ v$
Contraction	$(t \circ u) \circ u \sqsubseteq t \circ u$
Commutativity	$t \circ u \sqsubseteq u \circ t$

We won't prove the necessity and sufficiency of **all** the conditions, but we'll give the reader a clue about how such proofs go by providing one example:

Theorem 4.33 *DW is sound and complete for the class of models for which* $t \circ p \sqsubseteq q$ *only if* $t \circ q^\star \sqsubseteq p^\star$.

Proof: For soundness we need only verify that the contraposition axiom is valid, given the condition. To see this, note that contraposition is valid just if for all t, if $t \vDash A \to \neg B$, then $t \vDash B \to \neg A$. So suppose $t \vDash A \to \neg B$. To see that $t \vDash B \to \neg A$, we let $u \vDash B$ and show that $t \circ u \vDash \neg A$. To do this, in turn, we choose $t \circ u \sqsubseteq p \in P$ and show that $p^\star \nvDash A$. Since $t \circ u \sqsubseteq p$, there is $u \sqsubseteq r \in P$ so that $t \circ r \sqsubseteq p$. Thus $t \circ p^\star \sqsubseteq r^\star$. Since $u \vDash B$ and $u \sqsubseteq r$, $r \vDash B$. Thus $r^\star \nvDash \neg B$. So since $t \circ p^\star \sqsubseteq r^\star$, by horizontal heredity, $t \circ p^\star \nvDash \neg B$. So since $t \vDash A \to \neg B$, $p^\star \nvDash A$, as required.

For completeness we show that with the additional axiom in tow, the canonical model satisfies the condition. So suppose $t \cdot p \subseteq q$. To show that $t \cdot q^* \subseteq p^*$, let $B \in t \cdot q^*$. Then there is $A \in q^*$ with $A \to B \in t$. Since $A \in q^*$, $\neg A \notin q$. Thus since $t \cdot p \subseteq q$, $\neg A \notin t \cdot p$. Also, since $A \to B \in t$, $A \to \neg\neg B \in t$. So since $(A \to \neg\neg B) \to (\neg B \to \neg A)$ is an instance of the new axiom, $(\neg B \to \neg A) \in t$. So since $\neg A \notin t \cdot p$, $\neg B \notin p$. So $B \in p^*$. ∎

5 Variable Sharing

As mentioned in the introduction, the logics we're studying have features that plausibly suggest they are sensitive to *relevance*. This is true not only of **B**, which has been our focus so far, but of all the extensions of **B** introduced in the previous section. We'll now turn to describing this fact in more detail.

In particular, we'll prove that the strong relevant logic **R** (and thus every logic below it) has what has come to be known as the *variable sharing property* – if $A \to B$ is a theorem of this logic, then there is an atomic variable p that occurs in both A and B. We'll also show – and introduce the reader to one useful tool for showing – that this sort of content-sharing result can be strengthened.

5.1 Variable Sharing in **R**

The first of the results we will prove was proved, essentially, in Belnap (1960). It's worth noting, however, that what's *actually* proved in Belnap (1960) is a restricted form of the following result that holds only for sublogics of a certain sublogic of **R** known as **E**. The logic **E** was, when Belnap first published his result, one of the logics that relevant logicians were particularly interested in. But over the next couple of decades, relevance logicians became increasingly (though by no means exclusively) interested in **R**. Thus, in Anderson and Belnap (1975), Belnap's 1960 result was extended to apply to sublogics of **R** rather than sublogics of **E**. That said, the proof given in Anderson and Belnap (1975) is, mutatis mutandis, exactly the proof in Belnap (1960). So I think it's fair to say that the result was proved in the earlier paper. History aside, here's the result:

Theorem 5.1 (Variable Sharing) *If $A \rightarrow B$ is a theorem of **R**, then there is an atomic formula p that simultaneously occurs in both A and B.*

What we will actually do is follow Belnap and prove a stronger result that has the preceding theorem as a consequence. But first we need a definition:

Definition 5.2 *The sign of an occurrence of a formula A as a subformula of a formula B is defined as follows:*

- *The unique occurrence of A in A is a positive occurrence of A.*
- *If an occurrence of A in B or in C is positive (negative), the corresponding occurrence of A in $B \wedge C$ and in $B \vee C$ is positive (negative).*
- *If an occurrence of A in B is positive (negative), then the corresponding occurrence of A in $\neg B$ is negative (positive).*
- *If an occurrence of A in B is positive (negative), then the corresponding occurrence of A in $B \rightarrow C$ is negative (positive).*
- *If an occurrence of A in B is positive (negative), then the corresponding occurrence of A in $C \rightarrow B$ is positive (negative).*

To prove our main result in this section, we first prove a lemma that makes use of an eight-element partially ordered set called M_0 that looks like this:

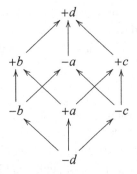

Where we interpret a directed arrow from x to y to mean that x is less than y. To interpret negation, we use the following chart:

A		$-d$	$-c$	$-b$	$-a$	$+a$	$+b$	$+c$	$+d$
$\neg A$		$+d$	$+c$	$+b$	$+a$	$-a$	$-b$	$-c$	$-d$

And to interpret the conditional, we use the following chart:

		$-d$	$-c$	$-b$	$-a$	$+a$	$+b$	$+c$	$+d$
$-d$		$+d$	$+d$	$+d$	$+d$	$+d$	$+d$	$+d$	$+d$
$-c$		$-d$	$+c$	$-d$	$+c$	$-d$	$-d$	$+c$	$+d$
$-b$		$-d$	$-d$	$+b$	$+b$	$-d$	$+b$	$-d$	$+d$
$-a$		$-d$	$-d$	$-d$	$+a$	$-d$	$-d$	$-d$	$+d$
$+a$		$-d$	$-c$	$-b$	$-a$	$+a$	$+a$	$+c$	$+d$
$+b$		$-d$	$-d$	$-b$	$-b$	$-d$	$+b$	$-d$	$+d$
$+c$		$-d$	$-c$	$-d$	$-c$	$-d$	$-d$	$+c$	$+d$
$+d$		$-d$	$-d$	$-d$	$-d$	$-d$	$-d$	$-d$	$+d$

An M_0-valuation is a function v from At to M_0. We can recursively extend any such function in exactly the same way we did when discussing MaGIC, viz. by elsewhere defining it via the following recursive clauses:

- $v(A \wedge B) = \inf\{v(A), v(B)\}$.
- $v(A \vee B) = \sup\{v(A), v(B)\}$.
- $v(\neg A) = M_\neg(v(A))$ where $M_\neg$ is given by the first chart above.
- $v(A \rightarrow B) = M_\rightarrow(v(A), v(B))$, where $M_\rightarrow$ is given by the second chart above.

Lemma 5.3 *If A is a theorem of $\mathbf{R}$ and v is an M_0 valuation, then $v(A) \in \{+a, +b, +c, +d\}$.*

Lemma 5.4 *If A and B don't share a signed variable, then there is an M_0-valuation v with the following features:*

- *If C occurs positively in A, then $v(C) \in \{-b, +b, +d\}$.*
- *If C occurs negatively in A, then $v(C) \in \{-b, +b, -d\}$.*
- *If C occurs positively in B, then $v(C) \in \{-c, +c, -d\}$.*
- *If C occurs negatively in B, then $v(C) \in \{-c, +c, +d\}$.*

Proof Sketch: The result is proved by explicitly constructing the valuation in question as follows:

if p occurs in A	and p occurs in B	then $v(p) =$
positively	not at all	$-b$
negatively	not at all	$+b$
not at all	positively	$+c$
not at all	negatively	$-c$
positively	negatively	$+d$
negatively	positively	$-c$

If p occurs neither in A nor in B then $v(p)$ can be chosen at random. From here the proof is by induction on the complexity of C, first for both "A" parts of the lemma at once, then for both "B" parts of the lemma at once. ∎

Theorem 5.5 (Strong Variable Sharing) *If $A \rightarrow B$ is a theorem of **R**, then there is an atomic formula p that occurs with the same sign in both A and B.*

Proof: Suppose A and B don't share a signed variable. Clearly A occurs positively in A. So where v is the valuation v defined in Lemma 5.4, $v(A) \in \{-b, +b, +d\}$. And since B occurs positively in B it follows for the same valuation that $v(B) \in \{-c, +c, -d\}$. Thus $v(A \rightarrow B) = M_\rightarrow(v(A), v(B)) = -d$, as one can see by inspecting the following fragment of the $M_\rightarrow$-chart:

	$-d$	$-c$	$+c$
$-b$	$-d$	$-d$	$-d$
$+b$	$-d$	$-d$	$-d$
$+d$	$-d$	$-d$	$-d$

Thus if A and B don't share a signed variable, then there is a valuation (namely v) that assigns $A \rightarrow B$ a value not in $\{+a, +b, +c, +d\}$. Thus by Lemma 5.3, if A and B don't share a signed variable, then $A \rightarrow B$ is not a theorem of **R**. ∎

Theorem 5.5 captures one way in which the logics we're looking at are "relevant" logics. In particular, to the extent that the atomic variables in a formula determine the *content* of the formula, each of the logics in the chart on page 26 contains a given conditional only if its antecedent and consequent share content.

Theorem 5.5 is the first and best-known example of a variable sharing theorem. But it's not the only such example. In the next section, I'll present another such result. I want to emphasize, however, that the tools used to prove the result in the next section are at least as important as the result itself.

5.2 Depth Substitution Invariance

I will state the results in this section with respect to the logics in the chart on page 26. But the results as I give are not in the most general possible form. Indeed, they are not even in the most general form *known*. One can find results holding for a broader range of logics in the literature – see, for example, Brady (1984a), Logan (2021), or Logan (2022b). That said, our focus here is on the results themselves and the methods used to prove them rather than on determining the precise range of logics for which the results hold and to which the methods can be applied. We begin, though, by situating the results we'll need.

Definition 5.6 *A substitution is a function σ mapping* At *to $\mathcal{L}^p$. We extend any such function to the whole language via the following recursive clauses:*

- $\sigma(\neg A) = \neg\sigma(A)$.
- $\sigma(A \wedge B) = \sigma(A) \wedge \sigma(B)$.
- $\sigma(A \vee B) = \sigma(A) \vee \sigma(B)$.
- $\sigma(A \rightarrow B) = \sigma(A) \rightarrow \sigma(B)$.

Definition 5.7 $X \subseteq \mathcal{L}^p$ is closed under substitutions *when, for all substitutions* σ, $\{\sigma(A) : A \in X\} \subseteq X$.

Lemma 5.8 *Each logic in the chart on page 26 is closed under substitutions.*

Lemma 5.8 should be in no way surprising – closure under substitution is typically taken to be a necessary condition for a logic's being properly *formal*. But there *is* a surprising result nearby for which we first need another definition:

Definition 5.9 *Let $\mathbb{N}$ be the set of natural numbers. A* depth substitution *is a function δ mapping* At$\times\mathbb{N}$ *to $\mathcal{L}^p$. We can extend such a function δ to a function* $\mathcal{L}^p \times \mathbb{N}$ *to $\mathcal{L}^p$ by the following recursive clauses:*

- $\delta(\neg A, n) = \neg\delta(A, n)$.
- $\delta(A \wedge B, n) = \delta(A, n) \wedge \delta(B, n)$.
- $\delta(A \vee B, n) = \delta(A, n) \vee \delta(B, n)$.
- $\delta(A \rightarrow B, n) = \delta(A, n + 1) \rightarrow \delta(B, n + 1)$.

We call these *depth* substitutions because they are substitutions that vary depending on how deeply nested within conditionals a given atom is. More concretely, we can define depth as follows:

Definition 5.10 *The depth of an occurrence of an atomic formula p as part of a formula A is defined recursively as follows:*

- *p occurs at depth 0 in its unique occurrence in the formula p.*
- *Given a depth n occurrence of p in A, the corresponding occurrences of p in $A \wedge B$, in $B \wedge A$, in $A \vee B$, in $B \vee A$, and in $\neg A$ are all depth n occurrences.*
- *Given a depth n occurrence of p in A, the corresponding occurrences of p in $A \rightarrow B$ and in $B \rightarrow A$ are depth $n + 1$ occurrences.*

Definition 5.11 $X \subseteq \mathcal{L}^p$ *is* closed under depth substitutions *when for all depth substitutions δ, $\{\delta(A, n) : A \in X \text{ and } n \in \mathbb{N}\} \subseteq X$.*

As an example of a depth substitution, consider the function δ defined by $\langle p_i, n \rangle \mapsto p_{i+n}$. If we let δ act on a formula in which some atom occurs in the scope of different numbers of conditionals, for example, $p_1 \rightarrow (p_1 \rightarrow p_1)$, then the scale of the weirdness of depth substitutions becomes apparent:

$$\delta(p_1 \rightarrow (p_1 \rightarrow p_1), 0) = \delta(p_1, 1) \rightarrow \delta(p_1 \rightarrow p_1, 1)$$
$$= p_2 \rightarrow (\delta(p_1, 2) \rightarrow \delta(p_1, 2))$$
$$= p_2 \rightarrow (p_3 \rightarrow p_3)$$

Just to emphasize how funky depth substitutions really are, notice what happened: the first occurrence of p_1 was replaced by an occurrence of p_2 and the other two occurrences of p_1 were replaced by occurrences of p_3. So one and the same atom – p_1 – has been replaced by different things in different occurrences within the same formula.

Lemma 5.12 *Let δ be a depth substitution and define δ' as follows:*

$$\delta'(p, n) = \begin{cases} \delta(p, n - 1) & \text{if } n > 0 \\ p & \text{otherwise} \end{cases}.$$

Then if $n > 0$, then $\delta'(A, n) = \delta(A, n - 1) \rightarrow \delta(B, n - 1)$.

Proof: By induction on the complexity of A. ∎

Corollary 5.13 *With δ' defined as just presented, $\delta'(A \rightarrow B, n) = \delta(A, n) \rightarrow \delta(B, n)$ for all $n \in \mathbb{N}$.*

Theorem 5.14 *Let Ax be one of the following axiom schemes defined on page 26: Suffixing, Prefixing, Contraction, or Commutativity. Suppose $X \subseteq \mathcal{L}^p$ meets the following conditions:*

- *X is closed under depth substitutions,*
- *X contains all instances of A → A,*
- *X contains all instances of Ax, and*
- *X is closed under R1.*

Then in fact X is trivial – which is to say X = $\mathcal{L}^p$.

Proof: By cleverly constructing a depth substitution that gets you in trouble.
∎

Corollary 5.15 *No logic above **DW** in the chart on page 26 is closed under depth substitutions.*

The point, at the end of the day, is that axioms like the ones listed in the theorem, when combined with closure under depth substitutions, R1, and essentially anything else at all are sufficient to drive us to triviality. The next theorem we'll prove is all the more remarkable in light of this. Before stating it, the reader should pause to verify the following lemma by a quick inspection of the axioms for the logics it mentions:

Lemma 5.16 *For A an axiom of either **DW** or **B**, δ a depth substitution, and $n \in \mathbb{N}$, $\delta(A, n)$ is an instance of the same axiom scheme as A.*

Theorem 5.17 (Depth Substitution Invariance) *Let **L** be either **DW** or **B**. Then if A is a theorem of **L**, δ is a depth substitution, and $n \in \mathbb{N}$, then $\delta(A, n)$ is a theorem of **L**.*

Proof: By induction on the length of the derivation of *A*. ∎

I want to emphasize just how bizarre a result this is. In some sense it shows that, so far as the weak relevant logics are concerned, the same atom *just can't* occur at different depths in a formula. Or perhaps better: while the formation rules in $\mathcal{L}^p$ don't prevent you putting the same atom at different depths in a given formula, the logic refuses to accept that occurrences of the same atom at different depths are in fact occurrences of the same atom.

Because the result is *so* odd, we'll take some time at the end of this section to say a bit more about it. For the time, however, let's turn to putting the result to work proving a stronger variable sharing theorem. The proof requires an injective (that is, one-one) depth substitution whose range includes only atomic formulae. Any such will do, but it's convenient to use the function *d* given by $d(p_i, n) = p_{2^i 3^n}$. Before stating our theorem, we need a lemma:

Lemma 5.18 *If all depth n occurrences of p_i in A are positive (negative), then for all m, every occurrence of $p_{2^i 3^{m+n}}$ in $d(A, m)$ is positive (negative).*

Theorem 5.19 *Let **L** be either **DW** or **B** and $A \rightarrow B$ be a theorem of **L**. Then some atomic formula p occurs in A and in B with (simultaneously) the same depth and the same sign.*

Proof: We prove the contrapositive. So, suppose that no variable p occurs with (simultaneously) the same depth and the same sign in both A and B. Then for all i and all n, if p_i occurs at depth n in both A and B, then either

(i) All depth n occurrences of p_i in A are positive and all depth n occurrences of p_i in B are negative, or

(ii) All depth n occurrences of p_i in A are negative and all depth n occurrences of p_i in B are positive.

The two cases are exactly parallel so we only deal with (i).

So, suppose (i) and consider $d(A, 1)$ and $d(B, 1)$. Suppose that some atom $p_{2^i 3^{1+n}}$ occurs in both. Then p_i occurs at depth n in both A and B. So by assumption, all depth n occurrences of p_i in A are positive and all depth n occurrences of p_i in B are negative. But then by Lemma 5.18, all occurrences of $p_{2^i 3^{1+n}}$ in $d(A, 1)$ are positive and all depth n occurrences of $p_{2^i 3^{1+n}}$ in B are negative. Thus, since every variable in $d(A, 1)$ and every variable in $d(B, 1)$ has the form $p_{2^i 3^{1+n}}$ for some i and some n, it follows that no variable occurs in both $d(A, 1)$ and $d(B, 1)$ with the same sign. Thus by Theorem 5.5 $d(A, 1) \rightarrow d(B, 1) = d(A \rightarrow B, 0)$ is not a theorem of **R**. So since $\mathbf{L} \subseteq \mathbf{R}$, $d(A \rightarrow B, 0) \notin \mathbf{L}$ either. But then by Theorem 5.17, $A \rightarrow B$ is not a theorem of **L** either. ∎

5.3 Depth Substitution, Philosophically

To my eyes Theorem 5.17 initially looks like a Bad Thing. It seems to be a fact about the language I actually use that I can use a given atomic sentence "p" in the scope of different numbers of conditionals and mean the same thing in each of its occurrences. Thus, to the extent that what we've just shown is that some of our favorite logics *don't* "think" that we *can* do that, they must, in some sense, be failing as models of theories built in the language we actually use.

In spite of the strength of this intuition, I've become convinced it's wrong. To see why, it helps to think about a slightly richer language than the one we've been using. To that end, we define the language $\mathcal{L}_a$ as follows:

- For each number n, $\mathcal{L}_a$ contains an atomic term $\bar{n}$.
- $\mathcal{L}_a$ contains the term-forming operators $+$, $\times$, and S governed by the following formation rules:
  - For any two terms τ and σ, $\tau + \sigma$ is a term.
  - For any two terms τ and σ, $\tau \times \sigma$ is a term.
  - For any term τ, $S\tau$ is a term.
- Given any two terms τ and σ, $\tau = \sigma$ is an atomic formula of $\mathcal{L}_a$.

But let's suppose that at this point, we continue just as we did in $\mathcal{L}^p$: atomic formulas are formulas, and we allow the formation of negations, conditionals, conjunctions, and disjunctions of formulas, all of which are also formulas.

This is a language in which we can express a certain amount of arithmetic. But if we consider arbitrary theories in this language, most of them do no such thing. Paying attention to this fact is helpful when thinking about Depth Substitution Invariance. To that end, consider two "interpretations" of $\mathcal{L}_a$:

- The standard interpretation, i_s, defined by saying $i_s(\bar{n}) = n$; that $i_s(\sigma + \tau)$ is the sum of $i_s(\sigma)$ and $i_s(\tau)$; that $i_s(\sigma \times \tau)$ is the product of $i_s(\sigma)$ and $i_s(\tau)$; and that $i_s(S\sigma)$ is the successor of $i_s(\sigma)$.
- The weird interpretation, i_w, defined by saying $i_w(\bar{n}) = n$ except that $i_w(\bar{5}) = 6$ and $i_w(\bar{6}) = 5$; that $i_w(\sigma + \tau)$ is the product of $i_w(\sigma)$ and $i_w(\tau)$; that $i_w(\sigma \times \tau)$ is the sum of $i_w(\sigma)$ and $i_w(\tau)$; and that $i_w(S\sigma)$ is the successor of $i_s(\sigma)$.

Now consider the theory, s, generated by $\{\sigma = \tau : i_s(\sigma) \text{ and } i_s(\tau) \text{ are the same number}\}$ and the theory, w, generated by $\{\sigma = \tau : i_w(\sigma) \text{ and } i_w(\tau) \text{ are the same number}\}$. Both s and w contain $\bar{2} + \bar{3} = \bar{5}$. But they do so for different reasons. Loosely speaking, s contains the sentence $\bar{2} + \bar{3} = \bar{5}$ because s "thinks" that "$\bar{2}$" means 2, "+" means plus, "$\bar{3}$" means 3, and "$\bar{5}$" means 5 while w contains the sentence $\bar{2} + \bar{3} = \bar{5}$ because w "thinks" that "$\bar{2}$" means 2, "+" means times, "$\bar{3}$" means 3, and "$\bar{5}$" means 6.

Now we'll make good on our digression: consider a formula in which $\bar{2} + \bar{3} = \bar{5}$ makes appearances at multiple depths. In such cases, our semantics allows that the formula may well be interpreted in one theory in one occurrence and in a different theory in another. Thus, for example, at one point in the evaluation, we might be interpreting "$\bar{2} + \bar{3} = \bar{5}$" as saying that two plus three is five, and in another point we might interpret it as saying that two times three is six. We really can't – in the *minimal* theory-building theory – rule out differences in interpretation of this scale. So we cannot have theorems – that is, entailments that are valid in the minimal theory-building theory – that *do* depend on interpreting the same atom in the same way when it occurs at two different depths. But the fact that this is impossible is exactly the content of the Depth Substitution Invariance theorem.

5.4 An Application of Variable Sharing

Variable sharing results are philosophically interesting. They're also heuristically useful. But they're more than just that; they can also be used to prove interesting things about relevant logics. We end this section by demonstrating one such thing: in weak enough logics, the theory generated by an atom (or the negation of an atom) is prime. Essentially this result was proved in Logan (2021), though we take the time here to work out its application to the case at hand, since that will end up being useful later in the Element.

We begin by defining a sort of normal form, then proving a normal form theorem for logics in the neighborhood of **DW**.

Definition 5.20 *An* intensional elementary conjunction *(iec) is a member of the smallest conjunctively closed set to contain*

- *Every atomic formula,*
- *Every negated atomic formula,*
- *Every entailment, and*
- *Every negated entailment.*

Clearly if A is an iec, then A is a finite conjunction of formulas of the four forms specified in the definition.

Definition 5.21 *An* intensional disjunctive normal *form (idnf) is a finite disjunction of iecs.*

Lemma 5.22 *For any sentence A and any logic L from the chart on on p. 26, there is an idnf A' so that $A \leftrightarrow A'$ is in L.*

Proof: By induction on the complexity of A. Only the conjunction case is interesting: if $A = A_1 \wedge A_2$, then by the inductive hypothesis, there are iecs $C_1^1, \ldots, C_1^{n_1}$ and $C_2^1, \ldots, C_2^{n_2}$ so that $A_1 \leftrightarrow (C_1^1 \vee \ldots \vee C_1^{n_1}) \in L$ and $A_2 \leftrightarrow (C_2^1 \vee \ldots \vee C_2^{n_2}) \in L$. From here induction on n_1 and n_2 finishes the job. ∎

Lemma 5.23 *Suppose L is either **DW** or **B**. Then*

- *If p occurs in A positively at depth 0, then for some formula A', either*

$-$ $A \leftrightarrow p \in \boldsymbol{L}$ *or*
$-$ $A \leftrightarrow (p \wedge A') \in \boldsymbol{L}$ *or*
$-$ $A \leftrightarrow (p \vee A') \in \boldsymbol{L}$; *also*

- *If p occurs in A negatively at depth 0, then for some formula A', either*
  $-$ $A \leftrightarrow \neg p \in \boldsymbol{L}$ *or*
  $-$ $A \leftrightarrow (\neg p \wedge A') \in \boldsymbol{L}$ *or*
  $-$ $A \leftrightarrow (\neg p \vee A') \in \boldsymbol{L}$.

Proof: By induction on the complexity of A, simultaneously in both parts. ∎

Lemma 5.24 *Let $\boldsymbol{L}$ be either $\boldsymbol{B}$ or $\boldsymbol{DW}$. Then if P is either an atomic formula or the negation of an atomic formula, A is an idnf, and B is an idnf, then $P \rightarrow (A \vee B)$ is a theorem of $\boldsymbol{L}$ only if either $P \rightarrow A$ or $P \rightarrow B$ is as well.*

Proof: We consider only the case where $P = p$ is an atom. Since p occurs positively at depth 0 in P, it follows by Theorem 5.19 that p occurs positively at depth 0 in $A \vee B$. Thus either p occurs positively at depth 0 in A or p occurs positively at depth 0 in B. We'll suppose the former, the argument for the latter being essentially identical.

To begin: since A is an idnf, there are iecs $C_1, \ldots, C_m$ so that $A = C_1 \vee \ldots \vee C_m$. Suppose C_i has n_i conjuncts and let $N_A = \max\{n_i\}_{i=1}^{m}$.

Since p occurs at depth zero in A, by Lemma 5.23, for some formula A', either

- $A \leftrightarrow p \in \mathbf{L}$ or
- $A \leftrightarrow (p \wedge A') \in \mathbf{L}$ or
- $A \leftrightarrow (p \vee A') \in \mathbf{L}$.

In the first case, $p \rightarrow A \in \mathbf{L}$, satisfying the requirement that either $p \rightarrow A$ or $p \rightarrow B$ be in $\mathbf{L}$. In the third case, since $(p \vee A') \rightarrow A \in \mathbf{L}$ and $p \rightarrow (p \vee A') \in \mathbf{L}$, transitivity for $\mathbf{B}$ gives that $p \rightarrow A \in \mathbf{L}$ again satisfying the requirement that either $p \rightarrow A$ or $p \rightarrow B$ be in $\mathbf{L}$. This leaves the second case, where $A \leftrightarrow (p \wedge A') \in \mathbf{L}$, to deal with.

Note first that since $A \rightarrow (p \wedge A') \in \mathbf{L}$ and $(p \wedge A') \rightarrow p \in \mathbf{L}$, transitivity for $\mathbf{B}$ gives that $A \rightarrow p \in \mathbf{L}$ as well. So $C_1 \vee \ldots \vee C_m \rightarrow p \in \mathbf{L}$. But for each i, $C_i \rightarrow (C_1 \vee \ldots \vee C_m) \in \mathbf{L}$ as well. So by transitivity for $\mathbf{B}$, for each i, $C_i \rightarrow p \in \mathbf{L}$. Thus by Theorem 5.19 again, for each i, p occurs positively at depth 0 in C_i. And since each C_i is an iec, it follows from this that each C_i either is p or contains p as a (proper) conjunct. From here the proof is a straightforward induction on N_A that we omit. ∎

Theorem 5.25 *Let **L** be either **B** or **DW**. Then if P is either an atomic formula or the negation of an atomic formula, then $P \rightarrow (A \lor B)$ is a theorem of **L** only if either $P \rightarrow A$ or $P \rightarrow B$ is as well.*

Proof: By Lemma 5.22, there are idnfs A' and B' so that $A \leftrightarrow A'$ and $B \leftrightarrow B'$ are in **L**. Since both $A' \rightarrow (A' \lor B')$ and $B' \rightarrow (A' \lor B')$ are instances of A4, transitivity gives that $A \rightarrow (A' \lor B')$ and $B \rightarrow (A' \lor B')$ are in **L**. So by A5, R2, and R1, $(A \lor B) \rightarrow (A' \lor B') \in \textbf{L}$. So since $P \rightarrow (A \lor B) \in \textbf{L}$, transitivity gives that $P \rightarrow (A' \lor B') \in \textbf{L}$. Thus by Lemma 5.24, either $P \rightarrow A'$ or $P \rightarrow B'$ is in **L**. Since $A' \rightarrow A$ and $B' \rightarrow B$ is in **L**, transitivity then gives that either $P \rightarrow A$ or $P \rightarrow B$ is in **L**.   ∎

We have, as an immediate corollary, a result we'll have need of later:

Corollary 5.26 *The theory generated by an atom or the negation of an atom is prime.*

5.4.1 A Discussion of the Result

Corollary 5.26 is a nice result that gives us a bit of a feel for the structure of the canonical model. But it's worth asking whether Theorem 5.25 says anything more than this. With a bit of a historical perspective, we can see that it does.

It helps to go back to an old debate in philosophical logic: the debate about whether logic should be *constructive*. We won't need to say a whole lot about this, other than to say that folks who preferred intuitionistic logic often preferred it because they said it *was* constructive, and folks who didn't care about constructiveness often favored classical logic instead. This is a gross oversimplification, but it'll do for our purposes.

A question worth asking is what, exactly, made intuitionistic logic seem constructive to the constructivists. And while there are a range of answers to this question, there are two results about intuitionistic logic that were both important to the discussion then and interesting in light of the preceding results. The first was proved in Gödel (1932):

Theorem 5.27 (Disjunction Property for Intuitionistic Logic) *If $A \lor B$ is a theorem of intuitionistic logic, then either A is a theorem of intuitionistic logic or B is a theorem of intuitionistic logic.*

The second, which is essentially the following, was proved in Harrop (1960):

Theorem 5.28 (Harrop's Rule for Intuitionistic Logic) *If $U \rightarrow (V \lor W)$ is a theorem of intuitionistic logic and no disjunction occurs positively in U, then* *either $U \rightarrow V$ is a theorem of intuitionistic logic or $U \rightarrow W$ is a theorem of intuitionistic logic.*

Both of these are taken to show some sort of "constructiveness" of intuitionistic logic. For the first, the idea is that a proof of $A \vee B$ must always in fact be either a proof of A or a proof of B. Proofs are thus constructive – you can always reconstruct, from a proof of a disjunction, which of the disjuncts is supported.

The second generalizes this to conditional provability. If you can prove that, were you given U, you could prove $V \vee W$, then – unless U is essentially disjunctive itself – you must be able to show that, were you given U, you could prove V or that, were you given U, you could prove W. As before, this seems to suggest that conditional provability – provability under assumption – is, in intuitionistic logic, also constructive.

Of note is that it's known that weak-enough relevance logics also satisfy the disjunction property. This was proved in Slaney (1984), though we (quite unfortunately) don't have space to go through the proof. Lemma 5.24 is, in some sense, a partial Harrop's rule for weak-enough relevance logics. Thus it suggests a yet further way in which these logics are constructive, which we take to be both technically and philosophically interesting.

5.4.2 Concluding Thoughts on Variable Sharing

In addition to the preceding results, there's been (and there continues to be) a lively community working on questions about how far results like these extend and how they are to be interpreted. As exemplars of the former we mention the work of Gemma Robles and José Méndez (see e.g. Méndez and Robles [2012] and Robles and Méndez [2014] to name just two pieces from a vast corpus) and the recent work of Damian Szmuc (see e.g. Szmuc [2021]). As an exemplar of the latter we mention the recent work of Ethan Brauer (see e.g. Brauer [2020]).

6 First-Order Models

We move now from our propositional language to a first-order language. Before diving in, here are a few details worth noting about our language: first, the language we will work in has exactly one quantifier – $\forall$. It will also, as usual, have countably many predicates of each arity, countably many variables $\{x_i\}_{i=1}^{\infty}$, and the connectives $\neg$, $\wedge$, $\vee$, and $\rightarrow$. As for the set of constants, we'll have reason to specify this very carefully in what follows, so for now I'll leave the matter to the side. Once constants are addressed, I'll take the reader to understand that the language(s) in question are constructed from the raw materials thus supplied in the usual ways. Finally, where A is a formula and σ and τ are terms, we write

$A(\sigma/\tau)$ to mean the formula one gets by replacing each free occurrence of σ with an occurrence τ.

6.1 Setup

Recall that each of the models we built in Section 3 models a collection of theories together with the operations, relations, distinguished points, and distinguished subsets that they naturally inherit. To begin to move from the propositional to the first-order level, we first define a zero-order frame to be a propositional frame together with a set N of constants. A zero-order model M is then a zero-order frame together with a function that maps each theory t to a function that, for all $i > 0$, maps each i-ary predicate P to a set $M_t(P)$ of i-tuples of constants. Zero-order models provide a very natural semantics for formulas in polyadic but unquantified (in the future, *zero-order*) languages $\mathcal{L}_N$ constructed using only members from N as constants. All we have to do is define $\vDash$ just as before, with the exception that in the atomic case we use the following clause:

- $t \vDash Pn_1 \ldots n_i$ if and only if $\langle n_1, \ldots, n_i \rangle \in M_t(P)$.

Now let's think about quantifiers. Given our perspective, the following "Tarskian" clause is not going to pass muster:

- If $\forall x A \in \mathcal{L}_N$, then $M_N, t \vDash \forall x A$ just if $M_n, t \vDash A(x/n)$ for all $n \in N$.

Of course, containing A instantiated at each constant really *is* a necessary condition on $\forall x A$ being in a theory. But it is also quite clearly insufficient. As an easy example: it is a fact about my own theory of the real numbers that (a) all the namable reals are namable, but also that (b) not all the reals are namable. Thus, when it comes to *theories*, the Tarskian clause just won't do the job – a predicate holding of all constants just doesn't entail the corresponding universal. What *does* guarantee that $\forall x A$ be in t is the following: take some constant ω not in the language of t. Then $\forall x A \in t$ if and only if $A(x/\omega)$ is in the theory generated by t in $\mathcal{L}_{N \cup \{\omega\}}$.

Before trying to make sense of this in the semantics, let's settle some notation. We assume that we have on hand a stock of ordinary constants, Con. Fix a countably infinite set $\Omega = \{\omega_i\}_{i=1}^{\infty}$ with $\text{Con} \cap \Omega = \emptyset$. For each finite set of numbers X, we write $\mathcal{L}_X$ for the language that takes the members of $\text{Con} \cup \{\omega_i\}_{i \in X}$ as available constants. We will think of the members of Con as ordinary constants and the members of Ω as additional constants that we *can* extend our language by.

In order to make sense of the idea that $\forall x A$ should be verified just if we can extend our language with a new constant ω at which $A(x/\omega)$ is verified, what we seem to need is not just *one* zero-order model but a whole *family* of zero-order models. Intuitively, we'll need, for each set X of constants we might add to our language, a frame F_X and model M_X on F_X that are meant to model the space of X-theories – that is, the space of theories in the language $\mathcal{L}_X$ defined in the previous paragraph.

But this isn't enough. We also need to be able to track when one theory is a "linguistic extension" of another, to borrow a phrase from Fine (1988). To do this, our models also need to include a function $\uparrow$ that assigns to each $t \in T_X$, and each pair $X \subseteq Y$, another theory $t\uparrow_X^Y$ that behaves like the theory generated by t in the language $\mathcal{L}_Y$. It also helps to include a function $\downarrow$ that goes in the other direction. At the level of theories, we think of $t\downarrow_X^Y$ – where now $t \in T_Y$ – as $t \cap \mathcal{L}_X$. All told, this means that the models we're going to build (stratified models) contain a multitude of zero-order models, and these internal models are linked up by the functions $\downarrow$ and $\uparrow$.

There is, however, one additional piece we need. Roughly, it says that our constants are just constants. They aren't special in any way. Thus, given any theory t and any two constants n and m in the theory of t, there should be a theory that extends t so as to make n and m indistinguishable. Nothing in the notion of a theory prevents any constant from behaving like any other. That's the idea. Formally, we model this by adding functions mapping T_X to T_X for each pair of constants n and m in $\mathcal{L}_X$. We diverge here from Fine's notation and write $[t]_m^n$ for the result of applying the $\langle n, m \rangle$-indexed function to t.

What remains is describing this all in enough detail that we can actually do something with it. We turn to that next.

6.2 Details

Let $\mathcal{F}$ be the set of finite sets of numbers, N be a countable set of constants, and $\Omega = \{\omega_i\}_{i=1}^{\infty}$ be a countable set disjoint from N. For $X \in \mathcal{F}$, we let $N \cup \{\omega_i\}_{i \in X} = N_X$. Then a stratified $\langle N, \Omega \rangle$-model has four parts:

- A function M from $\mathcal{F}$ to the set of zero-order models. We write M^X for the result of evaluating M at X and require M^X to be a model on the zero-order frame $F_X := \langle N_X, T_X, P_X, \ell_X, \circ_X, \sqsubseteq_X, \star_X \rangle$. We abuse notation slightly and write M_t^X for the various functions mapping i-ary predicates P to subsets of $(N_X)^i$.
- A set of functions $\downarrow_X^Y$ from T_Y to T_X, one for each $X \subseteq Y \in \mathcal{F}$,
- A set of functions $\uparrow_X^Y$ from T_X to T_Y, one for each $X \subseteq Y \in \mathcal{F}$, and

- A set of functions $[-]_X^{a,b}$ from T_X to T_X, one for each $X \in \mathcal{F}$ and each pair $\langle a, b \rangle \in (N_X)^2$.

N and Ω can often be determined contextually, so we will tend not to mention them. We will also almost always write just "$\sqsubseteq$" instead of "$\sqsubseteq_X$" since this too can usually be inferred from context. Finally, since stratified models have four parts, we will occasionally write them as 4-tuples of the following form:

$$\langle M, \{-\downarrow_X^Y\}_{X \subseteq Y \in \mathcal{F}}, \{-\uparrow_X^Y\}_{X \subseteq Y \in \mathcal{F}}, \{[-]_X^{a,b}\}_{a,b \in N_X} \rangle.$$

Each of these items corresponds to the intuitively described object of the same name in the preceding subsection.

So much for setup. The tricky part is saying how all of this machinery needs to interact. Let's start with the easy stuff. As mentioned in the previous section, for $X \subseteq Y$, the functions $\uparrow_X^Y$ and $\downarrow_X^Y$ are supposed to represent (respectively) the function that maps a theory in the language $\mathcal{L}_X$ to the theory it generates in the language $\mathcal{L}_Y$ and the function that maps a theory in $\mathcal{L}_Y$ to its $\mathcal{L}_X$-fragment. Given this, I'll take the need for the following three conditions to be fairly obvious:

(1) The down and up functions are covariant with the corresponding containment relations: if $t \sqsubseteq u$, then $t\downarrow_X^Y \sqsubseteq u\downarrow_X^Y$ and $t\uparrow_Y^Z \sqsubseteq u\uparrow_Y^Z$.

(2) The down and up functions are transitive: for $X \subseteq Y \subseteq Z$, $t\downarrow_Y^Z\downarrow_X^Y = t\downarrow_X^Z$, and $t\uparrow_X^Y\uparrow_Y^Z = t\uparrow_X^Z$.

(3) The models are conservative on predicates: for all $i > 0$, all i-ary predicates P, and all $t \in T_Y$, $M_{t\downarrow_X^Y}^X(P) = M_t^Y(P) \cap (N_X)^i$.

Moving on, we'll next discuss the following three conditions:

(4) For $t \in T_X$ and $X \subseteq Y$, $t\uparrow_X^Y\downarrow_X^Y = t$.

(5) For $t \in T_Y$ and $X \subseteq Y$, $t\downarrow_X^Y\uparrow_X^Y \sqsubseteq t$.

(6) $t\downarrow_{X \cap Y}^X\uparrow_{X \cap Y}^Y = t\uparrow_X^{X \cup Y}\downarrow_Y^{X \cup Y}$.

For (4), note that since t is already an $\mathcal{L}_X$-theory and $t\uparrow_X^Y$ is supposed to be the theory generated by t in $\mathcal{L}_Y$, it really ought to be the case that $t\uparrow_X^Y$ doesn't contain any $\mathcal{L}_X$-sentences not already contained in t. But this just means that if we restrict $t\uparrow_X^Y$ to its $\mathcal{L}_X$ fragment, then we arrive back at t. So $t\uparrow_X^Y\downarrow_X^Y$ really should be t, as (4) demands. If we reverse the order of these operations, however, it's possible that we lose information at the first step. So, as (5) says, $t\downarrow_X^Y\uparrow_X^Y$ should be a (perhaps improper) fragment of t.

The penultimate condition, (6), requires a bit more explanation. Roughly, what it says is this: given two languages $\mathcal{L}_X$ and $\mathcal{L}_Y$ that have some common fragment, either of the two obvious ways to turn an $\mathcal{L}_X$-theory into an $\mathcal{L}_Y$-theory get you to the same spot. In more detail, the "two obvious ways" in question are:

- Restrict from $\mathcal{L}_X$ to the common fragment first, then extend from there to $\mathcal{L}_Y$.
- Extend from $\mathcal{L}_X$ to a language that includes both $\mathcal{L}_X$ and $\mathcal{L}_Y$, then restrict to $\mathcal{L}_Y$ from there.

By inspection one can verify that $t\downarrow^X_{X\cap Y}\uparrow^Y_{X\cap Y}$ is the theory we get by following the first path and that $t\uparrow^{X\cup Y}_X\downarrow^{X\cup Y}_Y$ is the theory we get by following the second path. So, as promised, what (6) demands is that we get to the same place following either path.

Next we'll say a bit about how the primes behave:

(7) If $p \in P_Y$, then $p\downarrow^Y_X \in P_X$.

(8) If $p \in P_X, q \in P_Y, X \subseteq Y$, and $p \sqsubseteq q\downarrow^Y_X$, then for some $r \in P_Y, r\downarrow^Y_X = p$ and $r \sqsubseteq q$.

(9) If $t \in T_Y, X \subseteq Y$, and $t\downarrow^Y_X \sqsubseteq p \in P_X$, then for some $q \in P_Y, q\downarrow^Y_X = p$ and $t \sqsubseteq q$.

(10) If $p \in P_Y$ and $X \subseteq Y$, then $p^{\star_Y}\downarrow^Y_X = (p\downarrow^Y_X)^{\star_Y}$.

Recalling that the members of the various Ps are supposed to be prime, the need for (7) is clear: since $p \in P_Y$, p represents a prime. Intuitively, primes contain a disjunct of each disjunction they contain. Thus, in particular, for each $\mathcal{L}_X$-disjunction they contain an (ipso facto) $\mathcal{L}_X$-disjunct. So $p\downarrow^Y_X$ ought to be in P_X, as (7) requires.

Conditions (8) and (9), are (together) essentially the Lindenbaum Lemma in disguise. Seeing this essential equivalence is the sort of thing one can really only do after one sees the completeness proof – the reader who can't wait for the details should feel free to skip ahead to the argument on page 54.

To justify imposing condition (10), recall that intuitively $p^{\star_Y}$ contains exactly the $\mathcal{L}_Y$ sentences that p doesn't falsify. So what (10) demands is that the $\mathcal{L}_X$-fragment of the $\mathcal{L}_Y$-sentences that p doesn't falsify be exactly the same thing as the $\mathcal{L}_X$-sentences not falsified by p, which is as one would expect.

Next up we explain how the up and down functions interact with application and the logic:

(11) If $t \in T_X$, $u \in T_X$, and $X \subseteq Y$, then $(t \circ u){\uparrow}_X^Y = t{\uparrow}_X^Y \circ u{\uparrow}_X^Y$.

(12) If $t \in T_Y$, $u \in T_X$, and $X \subseteq Y$, then $(t \circ (u{\uparrow}_X^Y)){\downarrow}_X^Y \sqsubseteq t{\downarrow}_X^Y \circ u$.

(13) If $X \subseteq Y$, then $\ell_X{\uparrow}_X^Y = \ell_Y$.

Conditions (11) and (12) are again the sort of thing that's best understood only after having seen the completeness proof, so we'll leave them aside for now.

For (13), first note that the left-to-right containment follows from the basic idea of stratification, so it's really just the right-to-left containment that requires comment. For that, it suffices to note that we expect logics to be closed under both universal generalization and universal instantiation, which will suffice to give the result.

Penultimately we have the following conditions:

(14) $t \sqsubseteq [t]_X^{a,b}$.

(15) If $s \sqsubseteq t$, then $[s]_X^{a,b} \sqsubseteq [t]_X^{a,b}$.

(16) $[t]_X^{a,b} = [[t]_X^{a,b}]_X^{a,b}$.

(17) If $p \in P_X$, then $[p]_X^{a,b} \in P_X$.

(18) $[([p]_X^{a,b})\star x]_X^{a,b} = ([p]_X^{a,b})\star x$.

(19) $[t{\uparrow}_X^Y]_X^{a,b} = [t]_X^{a,b}{\uparrow}_X^Y$.

The first three of these are simply the demand that $[t]_X^{a,b}$ be a closure operator, (17) is self-explanatory, and (18) amounts to requiring that the dual of a symmetric set be symmetric. Condition (19), in turn says that the symmetrizing and extending operations commute. As with (8) and (9), it's easier to see why this should be the case after seeing the completeness proof.

The final three conditions are all fairly difficult. For the first two, we first need a definition:

Definition 6.1 *For $t \in T_X$ and a and b in N_X, we say that t is symmetric in a and b when a and b are indistinguishable in t. That is, when for all i-ary predicates P, $\langle n_1, \ldots, a, \ldots, n_i \rangle \in M_t^X(P)$ if and only if $\langle n_1, \ldots, b, \ldots, n_i \rangle \in M_t^X(P)$.*

With this notion in hand, here are two more fairly natural conditions:

(20) $[t]_X^{a,b}$ is symmetric in a and b.

(21) If $t \in T_X$ is symmetric in a and b, and $t \sqsubseteq p \in P_X$, then there is a $q \in P_X$ that is symmetric in a and b with $t \sqsubseteq q \sqsubseteq p$.

The last condition is important, so worth spending a moment on:

(22) If $a \in \{\omega_i\}_{i \in Y-X}$ and $b \in N_X$ then $[t \uparrow_X^Y]_Y^{a,b} \downarrow_X^Y \sqsubseteq t$.

Note what's going on here. Intuitively, $t \uparrow_X^Y$ is the theory generated by t in the Y vocabulary; a is one of the new constants we get when we extend to $\mathcal{L}_Y$ from $\mathcal{L}_X$; and b is one of the old constants. The theory $[t \uparrow_X^Y]_Y^{a,b}$ takes the theory generated by t in the Y vocabulary and extends it so that a and b are indistinguishable. $[t \uparrow_X^Y]_Y^{a,b} \downarrow_X^Y$ then restricts the result back to the X vocabulary. What we require is that in doing this, we don't gain any information about things in the X-vocabulary.

The idea is that we don't gain any new information by adding a new constant for something we've already named. We can do this, of course, and sometimes there are good reasons to do so. But simply calling something by two different names is not the sort of thing that should result in the production of new information. So if we look only at what we said about the old constant – which is essentially what "$\downarrow_X^Y$" asks us to do – we shouldn't find anything new.

And finally, truth conditions for the universal:

- If $\forall x A \in \mathcal{L}_X$, then $X, t \vDash \forall x A$ if and only if $X \cup \{i\}, t \uparrow_X^{X \cup \{i\}} \vDash A(x/\omega_i)$ for some $i \notin X$.

Note that this exactly captures our intuition about what it takes to verify that a given theory contains a universal: we need to check whether extending the theory with a new name (that is, with an ω_i for which $i \notin X$) gets us a theory that contains the formula instantiated at the new constant.

We complete the discussion by saying that $A \in \mathcal{L}_X$ is valid in a model M just if $M_X, \ell_X \vDash A$ and that A is valid when it is valid in all stratified models. We call the set of valid formulas **BQ**.

6.3 Important Results

There are four key lemmas to prove in order to demonstrate that models behave as they should. The first, horizontal heredity, is the stratified analogue of Lemma 3.2 from Section 3. As before, the purpose of this lemma is to show that the relation modeling containment actually gives a good model of containment. The second, the symmetry lemma, is there to check that symmetric theories really are symmetric. The third and fourth – downward heredity and upward heredity – essentially ensure the same sorts of containment demonstrated in the case of horizontal heredity, but in the "vertical" direction instead. Note that throughout we suppress as much notation as we can for the sake of readability. Where proofs are omitted it is because we think interested readers will be able to easily provide them.

Lemma 6.2 (Horizontal Heredity) *If $s \sqsubseteq t$ and $s \vDash A$, then $t \vDash A$.*

Lemma 6.3 (Symmetry Lemma) *If t is symmetric in a and b and A' is an a, b-variant of A, then $t \vDash A$ only if $t \vDash A'$.*

Lemma 6.4 (Downward Heredity) *If $A \in \mathcal{L}_X$ and $X \subseteq Y$, then $Y, t \vDash A$ if and only if $X, t\downarrow_X^Y \vDash A$.*

Proof: By induction on the complexity of A. Atoms are immediate from (3). Of the remaining cases, we deal with universals, leaving the rest to the reader.

Let $A = \forall x B$. For the "only if" direction, let Y, $t \vDash A = \forall x B$. Then there is $i \notin Y$ so that $Y \cup \{i\}$, $t\uparrow_Y^{Y \cup \{i\}} \vDash B(x/\omega_i)$. Thus, by the inductive hypothesis, $X \cup \{i\}$, $t\uparrow_Y^{Y \cup \{i\}} \downarrow_{X \cup \{i\}}^{Y \cup \{i\}} \vDash B(x/\omega_i)$. But by (6), $t\uparrow_Y^{Y \cup \{i\}} \downarrow_{X \cup \{i\}}^{Y \cup \{i\}} = t\downarrow_X^Y \uparrow_X^{X \cup \{i\}}$. Thus $t\downarrow_X^Y \uparrow_X^{X \cup \{i\}} \vDash B(x/\omega_i)$. And since $i \notin Y \supseteq X$, $i \notin X$. So $t\downarrow_X^Y \vDash \forall x B = A$.

For the "if" direction suppose instead that X, $t\downarrow_X^Y \vDash A$. Then there is $i \notin X$ so that $X \cup \{i\}$, $t\downarrow_X^Y \uparrow_X^{X \cup \{i\}} \vDash B(x/\omega_i)$. I claim that it follows that any $j \notin Y$ has this same feature. To see this, choose $j \notin Y$. Since by (4) $t\downarrow_X^Y \uparrow_X^{X \cup \{i\}} \uparrow_{X \cup \{i\}}^{X \cup \{i,j\}} \downarrow_{X \cup \{i\}}^{X \cup \{i,j\}} = t\downarrow_X^Y \uparrow_X^{X \cup \{i\}}$ the inductive hypothesis gives that $t\downarrow_X^Y \uparrow_X^{X \cup \{i\}} \uparrow_{X \cup \{i\}}^{X \cup \{i,j\}} \vDash B(x/\omega_i)$. But $t\downarrow_X^Y \uparrow_X^{X \cup \{i\}} \uparrow_{X \cup \{i\}}^{X \cup \{i,j\}} = t\downarrow_X^Y \uparrow_X^{X \cup \{i,j\}} = t\downarrow_X^Y \uparrow_X^{X \cup \{j\}} \uparrow_{X \cup \{j\}}^{X \cup \{i,j\}}$. Thus $t\downarrow_X^Y \uparrow_X^{X \cup \{j\}} \uparrow_{X \cup \{j\}}^{X \cup \{i,j\}} \vDash B(x/\omega_i)$. So by the Symmetry Lemma, $\left[t\downarrow_X^Y \uparrow_X^{X \cup \{j\}} \uparrow_{X \cup \{j\}}^{X \cup \{i,j\}}\right]^{\omega_i, \omega_j} \vDash B(x/\omega_i)(\omega_i/\omega_j) = B(x/\omega_j)$. Thus by the inductive hypothesis, $\left[t\downarrow_X^Y \uparrow_X^{X \cup \{j\}} \uparrow_{X \cup \{j\}}^{X \cup \{i,j\}}\right]^{\omega_i, \omega_j} \downarrow_{X \cup \{j\}}^{X \cup \{i,j\}} \vDash B(x/\omega_j)$. But by (22), $\left[t\downarrow_X^Y \uparrow_X^{X \cup \{j\}} \uparrow_{X \cup \{j\}}^{X \cup \{i,j\}}\right]^{\omega_i, \omega_j} \downarrow_{X \cup \{j\}}^{X \cup \{i,j\}} \sqsubseteq t\downarrow_X^Y \uparrow_X^{X \cup \{j\}}$. Thus by Horizontal Heredity, $t\downarrow_X^Y \uparrow_X^{X \cup \{j\}} \vDash B(x/\omega_j)$, as claimed.

So, choose $j \notin Y$ so that $X \cup \{j\}$, $t\downarrow_X^Y \uparrow_X^{X \cup \{j\}} \vDash B(x/\omega_j)$. By (6), $t\downarrow_X^Y \uparrow_X^{X \cup \{j\}} = t\uparrow_Y^{Y \cup \{j\}} \downarrow_{X \cup \{j\}}^{Y \cup \{j\}}$. So $t\uparrow_Y^{Y \cup \{j\}} \downarrow_{X \cup \{j\}}^{Y \cup \{j\}} \vDash B(x/\omega_j)$. Thus by the inductive hypothesis, $t\uparrow_Y^{Y \cup \{j\}} \vDash B(x/\omega_j)$. But then $t \vDash \forall x B = A$. $\blacksquare$

Lemma 6.5 *If $A \in \mathcal{L}_X$ then $X, t \vDash A$ if and only if $Y, t\uparrow_X^Y \vDash A$.*

Proof: By the previous lemma, $Y, t\uparrow_X^Y \vDash A$ if and only if $X, t\uparrow_X^Y \downarrow_X^Y \vDash A$. But since by (4) $t\uparrow_X^Y \downarrow_X^Y = t$, it then follows that $Y, t\uparrow_X^Y \vDash A$ if and only if $X, t \vDash A$, as required. $\blacksquare$

As with the final lemma of Section 3.1, our final lemma shows that ℓ_X really is the theory-building theory at play in the Xth stratum of the model:

Lemma 6.6 $X, \ell_X \vDash A \to B$ *if and only if for all* $t \in T_X$, *if* $X, t \vDash A$ *then* $X, t \vDash B$.

6.4 A Bit of Philosophical Reflection

Stratified models have *a lot* of moving pieces. It would be easy to lose sight of the philosophical significance of what we've seen. So let's pause for a minute to issue a few reminders. The point to keep in mind is this: stratified models are meant as models of spaces of theories. But when we ask what spaces of theories should look like in the first-order setting, there's an immediate problem.

Here's the scenario where the problem arises: someone hands you a set of sentences and, among them, is the sentence "everything is purple". You're then asked whether the set you've been handed is a theory. The problem, which you'll eventually realize, is this: you don't have enough information to answer the question! In particular, if "everything is purple" is among the sentences in the set, then a necessary condition on the set forming a theory is that for every constant c in the language of the theory, "c is purple" is also in the set. But in order to check whether this is so, you'd first need to know what the set of constants in the language of the theory *is*! Absent that information, you just *can't* say whether you've been handed a theory.

The kicker is that we can, of course, consider theories with different sets of constants – the space of constants is *indefinitely extensible* – we can always, if we want, add another constant to the set of constants we're using.

Altogether this gives us one good reason for using stratified models to deal with quantification: there really *isn't* just one all-encompassing space of theories to be modeling in the first place; there's a stratified hierarchy of spaces of theories. Working out the details from here, we end up seeing the following:

(a) Modeling the full space of first-order theories requires us to first stratify by languages, resulting in a stratification of our models.
(b) Having done this, we then have to equip these spaces of theories with machinery that tells us which theories are generated by which, which theories are restrictions of which, and which theories are treating some pairs of names as "stylistic" variants of each other.
(c) Finally, once we've got all of this on hand, all of the new machinery plays a role, spelled out previously, in telling us about the behavior of quantifiers.

Don't lose sight of the purpose of all this. In the end, whatever formulas are *valid* in the resulting class of models are formulas that *must be* endorsed by any theory-building practice that takes place in a first-order language. Put otherwise, the class of valid formulas implicitly specifies necessary conditions practices must specify if they are to count as theory-building practices at all. *That's* the philosophical payout, and I think it's sufficiently high-value to be worth tolerating a bit of complexity to get to. In the next section we start cashing in on it by axiomatizing the set of valid formulas.

7 Axiomatizing the First-Order Logic

Recall that **B** was axiomatized as follows:

A1. $A \to A$

A2. $(A \wedge B) \to A; (A \wedge B) \to B$

A3. $((A \to B) \wedge (A \to C)) \to (A \to (B \wedge C))$

A4. $A \to (A \vee B); B \to (A \vee B)$

A5. $((A \to C) \wedge (B \to C)) \to ((A \vee B) \to C)$

A6. $(A \wedge (B \vee C)) \to ((A \wedge B) \vee (A \wedge C))$

A7. $\neg\neg A \to A$

R1. $\dfrac{A \qquad A \to B}{B}$

R2. $\dfrac{A \qquad B}{A \wedge B}$

R3. $\dfrac{A \to B \qquad C \to D}{(B \to C) \to (A \to D)}$

R4. $\dfrac{A \to \neg B}{B \to \neg A}$

To axiomatize the set of valid formulas in stratified models, we add the following three axioms and one rule:

A8. $\forall x A \to A(x/\tau)$ where τ is free for x in A.

A9. $\forall x(A \to B) \to (A \to \forall x B)$ where x is not free in A.

A10. $\forall x(A \vee B) \to (A \vee \forall x B)$ where x is not free in A.

R5. $\dfrac{A(\omega)}{\forall x A(\omega/x)}$ where $\omega \in \Omega$.

Recall from the previous section that we will assume we have on hand both a countably infinite set of ordinary constants N and a countably infinite set $\Omega = \{\omega_i\}_{i=1}^{\infty}$ of additional constants we can extend our language with. In this section, we will specify that $\Omega = \text{Var}$. As before, so too here we identify, for each finite set of numbers X, the languages $\mathcal{L}_X$. This time, however, we can naturally interpret the members of $\mathcal{L}_X$ as the set of formulas in which only members of $\{x_i\}_{i \in X}$ occur freely. We will write $\mathcal{L}$ for the language $\mathcal{L}_N$. For convenience, we write Term_X for $\text{Con} \cup \{x_i\}_{i \in X}$.

With these different languages comes a natural "stratification" of the logic **BQ** itself. In particular, we will reserve the name **BQ** for the set of formulas provable using arbitrary $\mathcal{L}$-instances of the axioms and rules presented previously and write $\mathbf{BQ}_X$ for the subset of **BQ** containing only members of $\mathcal{L}_X$.

7.1 Addressing a Worry

Before going further, it's worth addressing a worry. Stated aloud, the worry usually goes something like this:

> Ok, so you've convinced me that the usual, "Tarskian" clause for the universal is problematic in our setting and that the clause you've given instead is more natural. All well and good. But does the Tarskian clause (perhaps unexpectedly) nonetheless do everything we need it to do?

The answer we can give to this question is less satisfactory than one might hope. In order to say what there is to be said, though, we first need to note that just as **B** could be extended in a variety of ways by restricting to models satisfying certain features, so also we can extend **BQ** by restricting the class of models appropriately. Explicitly, for each logic **L** listed in Section 4.2, we can build a corresponding logic **LQ** by restricting our attention to the stratified models built from zero-order models satisfying the corresponding conditions.

With that out of the way, here's the good news: for strong enough relevant logics, we know that the Tarskian clause is not only intuitively, but mathematically insufficient. More to the point, in Fine (1989), we have the following result:

Theorem 7.1 *The Tarskian semantics for first-order **RQ** validates formulas that are not provable in the axiomatic system for **RQ**.*

One way to respond to this, of course, is to say something along the lines of "so much the worse for the axiomatic system!". And while I'll admit sympathy to this, there are two problems. The first is that the axioms we've given previously *are*, one must admit, fairly natural as an axiomatic presentation of the first-order extensions of the logics we're interested in while, as already pointed out, Tarskian semantics isn't a particularly natural way to understand quantification here. Thus, confronted with the mismatch between what the Tarskian clause gets us and what the Hilbert system proves, it's more natural to blame Tarski than it is to blame Hilbert. Second, however, is that we simply don't know what the Tarskian clause gets us. We'll summarize this in the following:

Open Problem 1 *Where **L** is one of the usual relevant logics, is there a decent axiomatization of the set of formulas that are valid in the extension of **L** with Tarskian quantification?*

In fact, the situation is even more unsatisfactory than this suggests. First, the formula Fine produced as a witness to Theorem 7.1 is in no clear way revelatory of the mechanism behind the result. In fact, it's sufficiently complex that one expects there *has to be* a better example available. For the edification of the reader, here's the Tarski-valid but unprovable formula Fine found:

$$[(Pa \rightarrow \exists xEx) \wedge \forall x((Pa \rightarrow Fx) \vee (Gx \rightarrow Hx))] \rightarrow$$
$$[(\forall x(((Ex \wedge Fx) \rightarrow Qb) \wedge \forall y((Ey \rightarrow Qb) \vee Gy))) \rightarrow$$
$$[\exists Hx \vee (Pa \rightarrow Qb)]]$$

Having seen this, the reader likely understands the value of a solution to

Open Problem 2 *Is there a less-complex, more-illuminating formula that can witness Theorem 7.1? Barring that, can we explain why any such formula must bear this much complexity or, really, say anything intelligent at all about the general structure of such formulas?*

Second, unsatisfying as the example is for its complexity, it's also unsatisfying because it doesn't answer all the questions we'd like to see answers to. In particular, Fine's demonstration that the preceding formula is valid in **RQ** relies crucially on the assumption that the models he is working on at least contain the suffixing axiom. Thus, in particular, the following remains outstanding:

Open Problem 3 *Are **DW** and **B** incomplete for the Tarskian semantics?*

It's unfortunate that we're still in the dark on much of this. On the other hand, each of the preceding problems is readily accessible for anyone who manages to read this Element, and solution of any of them would be a valuable contribution to our understanding indeed.

7.2 Metatheory

Worry addressed, we return to doing metatheory. To get in the right state of mind – and because we'll have need of it in the following discussion – we encourage the reader to take the time to first prove the following lemmas:

Lemma 7.2 $BQ_X = BQ \cap \mathcal{L}_X$.

Lemma 7.3 *If $A \in \mathcal{L}_X$, $B \in \mathcal{L}_Y$, $Y - X = \{y_1, \ldots, y_n\}$, and $A \to B \in BQ_{X \cup Y}$, then $A \to \forall y_1 \ldots \forall y_n B \in BQ_X$.*

Lemma 7.4 *If $A \in \mathcal{L}_X$, $B \in \mathcal{L}_Y$, $Y - X = \{y_1, \ldots, y_n\}$, and $A \vee B \in BQ_{X \cup Y}$, then $A \vee \forall y_1 \ldots \forall y_n B \in BQ_X$.*

Lemma 7.5 (Transitivity for BQ) *If $A \to B \in BQ$ and $B \to C \in BQ$, then $A \to C \in BQ$.*

7.2.1 Soundness

As usual, the soundness proof is by induction on derivations.

Theorem 7.6 (Soundness for BQ) *If A is a theorem of BQ, then A is valid.*

Proof: By induction on the derivation of A. We deal only with A8, and leave the remaining cases to the reader.

For A8, it suffices to show that if $t \vDash \forall x A$, then $t \vDash A(x/\tau)$ provided τ is free for x. So, suppose $t \vDash \forall x A$. Then there is $i \notin X$ so that $X \cup \{i\}, t {\uparrow}_X^{X \cup \{i\}} \vDash A(x/\omega_i)$. It then follows by the Symmetry Lemma that $X \cup \{i\}, [t{\uparrow}_X^{X \cup \{i\}}]^{\omega_i, \tau} \vDash A(x/\omega_i)(\omega_i/\tau)$. But since τ was free for x in A, $A(x/\omega_i)(\omega_i/\tau) = A(x/\tau)$. So $X \cup \{i\}, [t{\uparrow}_X^{X \cup \{i\}}]^{\omega_i, \tau} \vDash A(x/\tau)$. Thus by Downward Heredity, $X, [t{\uparrow}_X^{X \cup \{i\}}]^{\omega_i, \tau} {\downarrow}_X^{X \cup \{i\}} \vDash A(x/\tau)$. But by (22), $[t{\uparrow}_X^{X \cup \{i\}}]^{\omega_i, \tau} {\downarrow}_X^{X \cup \{i\}} \sqsubseteq t$. So by Horizontal Heredity $X, t \vDash A(x/\tau)$ as required. ∎

7.2.2 Completeness

We again begin by giving a (somewhat less small) army of definitions.

Definition 7.7 *For $\Gamma \cup \{B\} \subseteq \mathcal{L}_X$, say that B X-follows from Γ – and write $\Gamma \vdash_X B$ – just if there is a sequence $A_1, A_2, \ldots, A_n = B$ so that for all i, either*

(a) $A_i \in \Gamma$ or
(b) there are $j < i$ and $k < i$ so that $A_i = A_j \wedge A_k$ or
(c) for some $j < i$, $A_j \to A_i \in BQ_X$.

Any such sequence is a X-derivation of B from Γ.

Definition 7.8 *We say that Γ is a formal X-theory when $\Gamma \vdash_X B$ just if $B \in \Gamma$. We write Th_X for the set of all formal X-theories.*

Definition 7.9 *For $s \subseteq \mathcal{L}_X$, the formal theory X-generated by s, $\|s\|_X$, is $\{B : s \vdash_X B\}$.*

Definition 7.10 Pr_X *is the set of all prime formal X-theories.*

Definition 7.11 *The* formal *X*-dual, s^{*X}, *of a set of formulas s is* $\{B \in \mathcal{L}_X : \neg B \notin s\}$.

Definition 7.12 *Given a formula* $A \in \mathcal{L}_X$, $a \in \mathrm{Term}_X$ *and* $b \in \mathrm{Term}_X$, *an* a, b-variant *of A is any formula we get by replacing some number of free a's in A with b's and some number of free b's in A with a's.*

Definition 7.13 *For* $\Gamma \cup \{B\} \subseteq \mathcal{L}_X$, $a \in \mathrm{Term}_X$ *and* $b \in \mathrm{Term}_X$, *say that B X-follows from* Γ *under the identification of a and b – and write* $\Gamma \vdash_X^{a,b} B$ *– just if there is a sequence* $A_1, A_2, \ldots, A_n = B$ *so that for all i, either*

(a) $A_i \in \Gamma$ *or*
(b) *there are* $j < i$ *and* $k < i$ *so that* $A_i = A_j \wedge A_k$ *or*
(c) *for some* $j < i$, $A_j \to A_i \in \mathbf{BQ}_X$ *or*
(d) *for some* $j < i$, A_i *is an* a, b-variant *of* A_j.

Any such sequence is an $X^{a,b}$-*derivation of B from* Γ.

Definition 7.14 Γ *is a formal* $X^{a,b}$-*theory when* $\Gamma \vdash_X^{a,b} B$ *just if* $B \in \Gamma$.

Definition 7.15 *For* $s \subseteq \mathcal{L}_X$, $a \in \mathrm{Term}_X$ *and* $b \in \mathrm{Term}_X$, *the formal theory X-generated by s under the identification of a and b,* $\|s\|_X^{a,b}$, *is* $\{B : s \vdash_X^{a,b} B\}$.

The canonical model is then the stratified $\langle \mathrm{Con}, \mathrm{Var} \rangle$-model corresponding to the following 4-tuple:

$$\langle CM, \{- \cap \mathcal{L}_Y\}_{Y \in \mathcal{F}}, \{\|-\|_Y\}_{Y \in \mathcal{F}}, \{\|-\|_Y^{a,b}\}_{Y \in \mathcal{F}}^{a,b \in \mathrm{Term}_Y} \rangle$$

where for each $X \in \mathcal{F}$, $CM^X = \langle \mathrm{Term}_X, \mathrm{Th}_X, \mathrm{Pr}_X, \mathbf{BQ}_X, \cdot, \subseteq, *_X \rangle$, and the functions CM_t^X map each i-ary predicate P to $\{\langle n_1, \ldots, n_i \rangle : Pn_1 \ldots n_i \in t\}$.

Philosophically, all this is as we should have hoped: in the canonical model, the theories are actual (formal) theories. The stratification of the theories is literally the stratification corresponding to the terms used in the theories. Extension to a larger language literally involves using the lower theory to generate a higher theory. Restriction to a small language literally involves restricting to a smaller vocabulary. And so on. In spite of this, there's a good deal of work left to be done. It's one thing, after all, to declare things to be what they ought to be and it's another thing to show that in so doing we've actually constructed what we say we've constructed – which is to say, what's left is showing that the canonical model is a stratified model, as intended.

A note: in the remainder of this section, we will essentially always omit "formal" from "formal theory", "formal application" and the like.

We begin with a few useful recharacterizations of the preceding notions:

Definition 7.16 *For $a \in \text{Term}_X$ and $b \in \text{Term}_X$, $\textbf{BQ}_X^{a,b}$ is the set of formulas axiomatized by the axioms and rules of $\textbf{BQ}_X$ together with the set of all formulas of the form $A \to A'$ where A' is an a, b-variant of A.*

Theorem 7.17 *The following are equivalent:*

(i) $A \vdash_X^{a,b} B$,
(ii) $A \to B \in \textbf{BQ}_X^{a,b}$, and
(iii) $A(a/b) \to B(a/b) \in \textbf{BQ}_X$.

Proof Sketch: The best way to go is to show that (i) entails (ii), (ii) entails (iii), and (iii) entails (i). For (i) entails (ii), the proof is a straightforward induction on the derivation of B from A. For (ii) entails (iii), prove instead something slightly more general: if $C \in \textbf{BQ}_X^{a,b}$, then $C(a/b) \in \textbf{BQ}_X$. This can be proved by a(n even more) straightforward induction on the derivation of C. Proving that (iii) entails (i) is then nearly immediate. ∎

Corollary 7.18 *$A \vdash_X B$ if and only if $A \to B \in \textbf{BQ}_X$*
Corollary 7.19 *For $t \in \text{Th}_X$, $\|t\|_X^{a,b} = \{B : A \to B \in \textbf{BQ}_X^{a,b}$ for some $A \in t\}$*

Note what this says about the notion of symmetry in play in stratified models. According to the corollary, symmetric theories are closed under the "logic" $\textbf{BQ}_X^{a,b}$. In this logic, any two a, b-variants of the same formula are equivalent. Thus, for example, $Faa \to Fba$ and $Fba \to Fab$ are both theorems of $\textbf{BQ}_X^{a,b}$. One might naturally wonder, then, what exactly symmetry is capturing.

Fine, when introducing these matters, had the following to say about it, where I've adjusted his syntax mildly to fit ours:

> imagine that a and b are merely typographic variants of one another; one would then want to treat A and its variants as if they were the same formula.

The point Fine is making here is worth taking quite seriously: in a theory that is symmetric in a and b, a and b aren't being treated (merely) as coreferential terms or terms that in some other way "mean" the same thing. Instead, they're being treated as literally the same term. The identity being imposed is (borrowing language from Logan and Leach-Krouse [2021]) an identity *at the level of syntax*. The fact that stratified semantics depends so heavily on this notion seems, to me, worthy of more serious philosophical investigation than it has received to date. But that's not within our remit to say more about, so we move on.

Lemma 7.20 *If t is an $X^{a,b}$-theory, Δ is closed under disjunctions and $t \cap \Delta = \emptyset$, then there is a prime $X^{a,b}$-theory $p \supseteq t$ with $p \cap \Delta = \emptyset$*

Corollary 7.21 *If t is an X-theory, Δ is closed under disjunctions and $t \cap \Delta = \emptyset$, then there is a prime X-theory $p \supseteq t$ with $p \cap \Delta = \emptyset$*

Lemma 7.22 *Each F_X is a frame.*

Lemma 7.23 *The canonical stratified model is a stratified model.*

Proof: There are 22 conditions to verify. We will check only conditions 8 and 19. The remainder are left to the reader.

For condition (8): We need to show that if $p \in \text{Pr}_X$, $q \in \text{Pr}_Y$ and $p \subseteq q \cap \mathcal{L}_X$, then there is $r \in \text{Pr}_Y$ so that $r \cap \mathcal{L}_X = p$ and $r \subseteq q$. To begin, let $Y - X = \{y_1, \ldots, y_k\}$, $\bar{p} = \mathcal{L}_X - p$ and $\bar{q} = \mathcal{L}_Y - q$. Finally, let $\Delta = \bar{p} \cup \bar{q}$ and Δ' be the smallest disjunctively closed set to contain Δ. Since p and q are prime, $\bar{p}$ and $\bar{q}$ are closed under disjunction. So there are three types of formulas in Δ':

- Formulas that are in $\bar{p}$,
- Formulas that are in $\bar{q}$, and
- Formulas that are equivalent to a formula of the form $D_p \vee D_q$ with $D_p \in \bar{p}$ and $D_q \in \bar{q}$.

From here the idea is to show that $\| p \|_Y \cap \Delta' = \emptyset$, then apply the Lindenbaum Lemma to extend $\| p \|_Y$ away from Δ'. The result will be a prime r that contains p (because it contains $\| p \|_Y$), contains nothing in $\bar{p}$ (because it won't intersect $\Delta' \supseteq \bar{p}$), and also contains nothing in $\bar{q}$. It will follow from the first two facts that $r \cap \mathcal{L}_X = p$ and from the third that $r \subseteq q$, as required.

To see that $\| p \|_Y \cap \Delta' = \emptyset$, note first that since $p \subseteq q \cap \mathcal{L}_X$, $\| p \|_Y \cap \bar{p} = \emptyset$ and $\| p \|_Y \cap \bar{q} = \emptyset$. So all we need to show is that no formula of the third type is in $\| p \|_Y$. For this, in turn, it suffices to show that no formula that *is* of the given form is in $\| p \|_Y$, since this happens if and only if a formula equivalent to a formula of this form is in $\| p \|_Y$.

Our proof is by contradiction. So, suppose that $D_p \in \bar{p}$, $D_q \in \bar{q}$, and $D_p \vee D_q \in \| p \|_Y$. Then by Corollary 7.18, for some $A \in p$, $A \rightarrow (D_p \vee D_q) \in \mathbf{BQ}_Y$. But since A and D_p are both in $\mathcal{L}_X$ careful application of Lemma 7.3 and Lemma 7.4 gives that $A \rightarrow (D_p \vee \forall y_1 \ldots \forall y_k D_q) \in \mathbf{BQ}_X$. So since $A \in p$, $D_p \vee \forall y_1 \ldots \forall y_k D_q \in p$. And then since p is prime we must have that either $D_p \in p$ or $\forall y_1 \ldots \forall y_k D_q \in p$. But since $D_p \in \bar{p}$, $D_p \notin p$. And since $p \subseteq q \cap \mathcal{L}_X$, if $\forall y_1 \ldots \forall y_k D_q \in p$, then $\forall y_1 \ldots \forall y_k D_q \in q$. But then $D_q \in q$, which is impossible since $D_q \in \bar{q}$. So $\|p\|_Y \cap \Delta' = \emptyset$ and the Lindenbaum Lemma finishes the job.

For condition (19): we need to show that if $t \in \mathrm{Th}_X$, then $\|\|\|t\|_Y\|_Y^{a,b} = \|\|\|t\|_X^{a,b}\|_Y$. We do this by proving containment in each direction separately. For left to right, let $C \in \|\|\|t\|_Y\|_Y^{a,b}$. Then there are $A \in t$ and $B \in \mathcal{L}_Y$ so that $A \rightarrow B \in \mathbf{BQ}_Y$ and $B \rightarrow C \in \mathbf{BQ}_Y^{a,b}$. Thus $A \rightarrow C \in \mathbf{BQ}_Y^{a,b}$. So, letting $Y - X = \{y_1, \ldots, y_k\}$, since $A \in t$, $A \rightarrow \forall y_1 \ldots \forall y_k C \in \mathbf{BQ}_X^{a,b}$. Thus $\forall y_1 \ldots \forall y_k C \in \|t\|_X^{a,b}$. So $C \in \|\|\|t\|_X^{a,b}\|_Y$.

For right to left, let $C \in \|\|\|t\|_X^{a,b}\|$. Then by Lemma 7.18 there is $B \in \mathcal{L}_X$ and $A \in t$ so that $A \rightarrow B \in \mathbf{BQ}_X^{a,b} \subseteq \mathbf{BQ}_Y^{a,b}$ and $B \rightarrow C \in \mathbf{BQ}_Y \subseteq \mathbf{BQ}_Y^{a,b}$. So $A \rightarrow C \in \mathbf{BQ}_Y^{a,b}$. And thus, since $A \in t \subseteq \|t\|_Y$, $C \in \|\|\|t\|_Y\|_Y^{a,b}$. ∎

Finally, we show that containment and commitment agree.

Lemma 7.24 *For $A \in \mathcal{L}_X$ and $t \in \mathrm{Th}_X$, $X, t \vDash A$ if and only if $A \in t$.*

Proof: By induction on A. Here is one direction of the quantificational cases; everything else being left to the reader:

Suppose $X \cup \{x_i\}, \|t\|_{X \cup \{x_i\}} \vDash B(x_i)$. Then by the inductive hypothesis, $B(x_i) \in \|t\|_{X \cup \{x_i\}}$. Thus by Lemma 7.18, for some $A \in t \subseteq \mathcal{L}_X$, $A \rightarrow B(x_i) \in \mathbf{BQ}_{X \cup \{x_i\}}$. So by Lemma 7.3, $A \rightarrow \forall x_i B(x_i) \in \mathbf{BQ}_X$. Thus $\forall x_i B(x_i) \in t$. ∎

From here our completeness proof finishes in the expected way.

Theorem 7.25 *If A is valid in stratified models, then $A \in \mathbf{BQ}$.*

Proof: Suppose $A \notin \mathbf{BQ}$. Then by Lemma 7.24, A is not valid in the canonical model. So since by Lemma 7.23 the canonical model is a stratified model, A is not valid in stratified models. ∎

8 A Very Biased and Very Partial Survey of Some Other Topics in the Area

This Element is short and presents only one perspective on a few small parts of what is a rather large and dynamic field of research. In this section, I present a brief survey of some other topics and perspectives. For each, I also point to useful places in the literature where more detailed treatments are available.

As the section heading suggests and I hereby acknowledge, my own biases are very much present in both the selection of topics covered and the particular ways I've chosen to cover them. The reader looking for a guide to the terrain is advised to keep this in mind.

8.1 Alternative Semantic Theories

I've focused my attention in this Element on Fine-style binary-operational semantics for relevance logics. But among semantic theories for relevant logics, Fine-style semantic theories are decidedly *not* the most popular choice. That honor goes without question to the ternary relational semantics first pioneered by Richard Sylvan (nee Routley) and Robert K. Meyer in Routley and Meyer (1972a, 1972b, 1972c).

In addition to ternary relational semantics, however, relevance logics enjoy at least three other interesting semantic theories. The first is a newcomer – the *collection frame* semantics presented in Restall and Standefer (2022). The second is Ross Brady's content-inclusion semantics pioneered in Brady (1988, 1989). The third is the algebraic semantics via De Morgan monoids, presented by Dunn in (among other places) §28.2 of Anderson and Belnap (1975). Because of – and only because of! – space considerations, we'll only have a very small amount to say about the latter two.

8.2 Ternary Relations

The heart of the difference between ternary relational semantics and the Fine-style operational semantics we've been considering here concerns disjunction. Rather than the clause we've been using in the Element so far, namely

$t \vDash A \vee B$ if and only if $p \vDash A$ or $p \vDash B$ for all $t \sqsubseteq p \in P$,

the ternary-relationist instead uses the following more "classical" looking clause:

$t \vDash A \vee B$ if and only if $t \vDash A$ or $t \vDash B$.

This is a significant simplification, and it cascades to allow further simplifications in the remainder of the semantics. To see why note that one of the consequences of this change of clauses is that *every* point – and not just a special subset of the points – will be prime. Thus, rather than specifying both the set of theories and the subset consisting of the primes, this choice allows us to define our models on a single set – intuitively the set of primes – all of which have a dual. So the $\star$ operation can be taken to be total rather than partial. The change in semantic clause for disjunction is thus at least three simplifications rolled into one.

Unfortunately, there are also a few complications that come along with the change. One particularly important complication concerns the application operation. The problem in a nutshell is that a prime applied to a prime isn't always a prime. As an example: first note that $(A \rightarrow (B \vee C)) \rightarrow ((A \rightarrow B) \vee (A \rightarrow C))$ isn't a theorem of **B**. So the theory – let's call it t – generated by $A \rightarrow (B \vee C)$ doesn't contain $(A \rightarrow B) \vee (A \rightarrow C)$. Thus there is a prime – let's call it p – that extends t that doesn't contain $(A \rightarrow B) \vee (A \rightarrow C)$. So p also doesn't contain $A \rightarrow B$ and doesn't contain $A \rightarrow C$.

Now suppose that A is an atom. Then as per Theorem 5.25 in Section 5, the theory – let's call it s – generated by A is prime. So here's what we have: p, being an extension of t, contains $A \rightarrow (B \vee C)$. And s, being generated by A, clearly contains A. So if we apply p to s, the resulting theory contains $B \vee C$. But since p contains neither $A \rightarrow B$ nor $A \rightarrow C$, the theory we get by applying p to s contains neither B nor C. So the theory we get when we apply the prime theory p to the prime theory s is not itself a prime theory. Thus application isn't well defined when restricted to primes.

The solution to this problem adopted by the ternary relation semanticists is really quite clever. First, view the binary operation as a three-place relation in the usual way – that is, think of it as the three-place relation "s applied to t equals u." Now notice that, while this relation doesn't do the work we need when we restrict our attention to primes, there's a natural nearby candidate that does, namely the relation "s applied to t is contained in u."

In fact, there's more: given that the behavior of a theory is determined entirely by the behavior of the primes that extend it, this relation loses none of the information present in the more general binary operational setting. So one expects (and, indeed, finds) that redoing all the semantics from the preceding discussion using this relation will yield the same results. This has been worked out in detail in various places. The first such working-out was in the trio of papers by Routley and Meyer (1972a, 1972b, 1972c). Textbook treatments of this perspective include both Read (1988) and Mares (2004). Extension of the resulting perspective to the setting of first-order logic was gestured at in Fine (1988) and fleshed out more thoroughly in Logan (2019).

That said, while everything does in fact work, there are definite downsides to using a single three-place relation $Rxyz$ instead of using both a binary operation and a binary containment relation. Consider, for example, the definition of associativity. To say that application is associative is to say that $(s \circ t) \circ u = s \circ (t \circ u)$. But in ternary relation land we can't talk about *the* application of one theory to another. Instead we have to talk about those primes that extend the application of one theory to another. Thus, instead of talking about "$s \circ t$" we instead talk about the set of all primes that extend the application of s to t – that is, all those z so that $Rstz$. And instead of $(s \circ t) \circ u$ we instead talk about all the primes that extend something that we get by applying to u something that extends the application of s to t – that is, all those w so that for some z, $Rstz$ and $Rzuw$. Similar rephrasing is required to deal with $s \circ (t \circ u)$. Altogether then, to say that application is associative, we say the following:

> For all s, t, and u, if for some z we have that both $Rstz$ and $Rzuw$, then for some y we have that both $Rsyw$ and $Rtuy$.

As this hopefully makes clear, a great many things that are easy to say using binary operations are quite difficult to say using ternary relations. Recently, ternary relationists have discovered that this particular problem – the problem of things being harder to say than they should be – is one that can be sidestepped by generalizing ternary relational semantics just a bit. We turn to that generalization in the next subsection. Before doing that, however, we present one further problem that *isn't* sidesteppable in the same way.

The long and the short of the problem is that some of the strong relevant logics are themselves nonprime. For example, the logic **R** has all instances of $A \lor \neg A$ as theorems. But there are some formulas – for example, the atoms – for which neither A nor $\neg A$ are theorems. But this means that when we restrict our attention to primes alone, the logic itself fails to occur among the theories we're looking at. Semantically, this leaves us without a "base point" on which to evaluate whether a formula belongs to the logic.

I should be completely clear about the charge I'm leveling – the problem isn't that we can't deal with strong relevant logics using a semantics in which we check for validity in a model by examining a single point – this *can be* done, and was in fact the way of doing things that kicked the whole thing off in Routley and Meyer's initial investigation. The point is that we're left without points in our models where *exactly* the theorems of the logic are validated.

As with the issue of $\circ$ being undefined, this problem too can be addressed if we're willing to complicate our models sufficiently. This time, the idea is to replace the single base point ℓ in a model with a class of "normal points," each intuitively representing a prime extension of the logic. To determine what's in the logic, then, we simply look to see what's in every normal point.

Technically, this does the trick. But there's a bit of unease left – one wants to know why the logic itself isn't good enough to count. Or, perhaps more helpfully, one wants to know what exactly we should understand our models to be modeling such that all of the following are simultaneously on the table:

- Some of the things being modeled are inconsistent – they verify, for some A, both A and $\neg A$.

- Some of the things being modeled are incomplete – they verify, for some A, neither A nor $\neg A$.
- All of the things being modeled are prime – they verify $A \vee B$ only if they verify either A or B.
- One *can* single out a subclass of the things being modeled that are, in some way "normal," but
- The thing that all the normal things have in common *isn't* among the things being modeled.

As an authorial aside, I'll note that the (to me seemingly insuperable) difficulty of coming up with something worthy of serious philosophical attention that meets all five of these conditions at once is what led me away from ternary relations and into the welcoming arms of binary operations. But ternary relations remain widely embraced, so the reader should make their own judgment of their merits.

One downside (for the ternary relationist at least) of the popularity of ternary relation semantics is that very nearly every attack on the semantics of relevant logics has been an attack aimed squarely at ternary relations. In this vein, some of the important works are those of Copeland (see Copeland [1979] and Copeland [1980]) and Brady (2017b).

Historical Aside: I'm presenting things as if ternary relation semantic theories were developed *after* binary operational theories were. In fact that's not the case; the two theories were developed roughly simultaneously. But a bit of anachronism makes the story easier to tell. Hopefully this mea culpa is sufficient penance.

8.3 Collection Frames

As mentioned earlier, Greg Restall and Shawn Standefer have recently provided a novel semantic theory that addresses some of the difficulties involved with ternary relations. The basic idea of the theory – presented in Restall and Standefer (2022) – is to replace the ternary relation $Rabc$ with a binary relation relating collection-like objects composed of points to points.

We'll restrict our attention here to the application of their framework to our preferred logic **B** – though the reader should be aware that their approach applies much more broadly. In addition, we will follow Restall and Standefer in restricting our attention to the negation-free fragment of **B**.

Restrictions in place, the idea is this: rather than spelling out the semantics using a three place relation, they instead use a binary relation relating binary trees of points to points. This, it turns out, is a spectacularly successful way to generalize the idea at the heart of ternary relation semantics.

To say more, let's first explain how to read a binary tree of points as shorthand for a compositional description of a particular point. Before that, let's give a concrete definition of the set of binary trees of points:

Definition 8.1 *If X is a set, a binary X-tree is a directed tree whose leaf nodes are all labeled with members of X. We identify the simplest binary X-trees – those that consist of a single node with no edges – with members of X in the obvious way.*

Definition 8.2 *If X is a set and $\circ$ is a binary operation on X, then we define the function i mapping binary X-trees to members of X as follows:*

- *For $t \in X$, $i(t) = t$.*
- *If T has the form $T_1 \diagdown \quad \diagup T_2$, then $i(T) = i(T_1) \circ i(T_2)$.*

Thus, for example, the interpretations of $x \diagdown \quad \diagup y \quad z$ and of $x \quad y \diagdown \quad \diagup z$

are $(x \circ y) \circ z$ and $x \circ (y \circ z)$, respectively.

Of course, the application-case we have in mind for trees and interpretations of trees is the case where the set X is the set of theories in some model and the binary operation is the application operation. With all of this in hand, here's how to understand Restall and Standefer's semantics from the operational perspective: just as ternary relation semantics replaces the binary operation $\circ$ and binary relation $\sqsubseteq$ with a single ternary relation that captures the content of "$a \circ b \sqsubseteq c$," Restall and Standefer have built a semantics that instead replaces them with a binary relation that captures the content of "$i(T) \sqsubseteq c$," which they take as a semantic primitive in their system.

This is, it must be admitted, a rather ingenious bit of formalism. What's more is that the various generalizations of it that Restall and Standefer introduced in their paper completely solve the "things are harder to say than they should be" family of problems. The observation to make is that (in more ways than we have space here to cover) the particular identity of the objects that fill the left-hand spot in the just mentioned binary relation are unimportant to the functioning of the semantics. Thus, rather than *imposing* things like associativity by adopting new semantic postulates, one can simply replace "nonassociative objects" like trees with more obviously "associative objects" in the preceding construction and arrive at the same result.

Here's what I mean: suppose instead of using trees, we instead used lists of points. Lists are associative in the sense that the natural list-combining operation of *concatenation* is itself associative: if we first append the list l_2 to the list l_1 and then append l_3 to the resulting list, the result is the same as if we'd first appended l_3 to l_2 and then appended this list to l_1. Thus, the natural generalization to lists of the notion of interpretation given earlier is an associative notion. The binary relation "the (generalized) interpretation of L is contained in c" then automatically carries associativity with it.

This sidesteps the issue of things being harder to say than they should be, and sidesteps it in the most elegant way possible – it simply leaves us with no reason to even say in the first place the things that were hard to say. To work in an associative logic just is to work in a logic where the objects in the left-hand spot of the binary relation being considered are associative objects. One doesn't need to say anything at all to make this happen, so one certainly needn't say something that is harder to say than it needs to be.

8.4 Concluding Thoughts and Other Approaches

Both the genuinely ternary approach to the semantics of relevant logics and its binary cousin in collection frames are rather clever and allow the use of a more familiar looking clause for disjunction. But the former is plagued by several problems and while the latter solves one, it leaves the others untouched. Both also leave unanswered a range of questions about why one ought to avoid nonprimes in the first place. But provided these are things one wants to (or at least can) live with, each provides a genuinely interesting approach to the semantics of relevance logics.

As mentioned at the start of this section, there are other options as well. Worth mention are two that have seen a fair amount of development. The first is the content semantics mostly associated with the work of Ross Brady. This has seen its most detailed development in Brady (2006), to which the interested reader is referred.

In brief the idea is this: relevance, intuitively, has something to do with inclusion of content. Rather than cooking up logics in some other sense, then showing that the resulting systems have nice content-inclusion features, Brady's idea is to go straight to the punchline and build a semantics that explicitly bakes in contents, and to then define validity directly in terms of content containment.

One has to admire the directness of the approach. Given one has an interest in content containment, it's also in some sense the *right* approach. That said, the technical complications the approach requires place it beyond the scope of the current discussion.

Another important branch of research in this area concerns algebraic semantics. The basic idea is to find an algebraic object that plays the role for relevance logics that boolean algebras play for classical logic. That this can be done nicely is surprising. That the resulting algebraic perspective generalizes to the first-order setting is even more surprising. But the former has been the subject of a range of investigations (see e.g. the seminal work by Dunn in §28.2 of Anderson and Belnap [1975]) and the latter has been demonstrated in work of Andrew Tedder that is, as of this writing, forthcoming. The algebraic approach has also led to a rich and mathematically interesting generalization in the form of gaggle theory, as developed most fully in Bimbó and Dunn (2008).

We'll end by briefly mentioning two additional avenues of semantic development. The first is the alternative semantics for relevant quantification provided by Mares–Goldblatt in Mares and Goldblatt (2006). Those looking for an interesting project to work on might consider the problem of stating the exact relation between Mares–Goldblatt semantics and stratified semantics which is, as of this writing, not well understood. The second is the approach to the semantics of relevant logics using "neighborhoods." These theories augment ternary-relational models with a sets of theories called "propositions." Routley and Meyer (1975a, 1975b) are the original instances of this approach; for recent work see Goble (2003), Standefer (2019), Tedder (2021), Ferenz and Tedder (2022), and Tedder and Ferenz (2022).

8.5 Alternative Proof Theories

In addition to alternative semantic theories, relevant logics can be equipped with a variety of different proof systems. In the preceding discussion, all of the logics we surveyed were given Hilbert-style axiomatizations. These are acceptable for the purposes of the Element, but leave a lot to be desired in terms of intelligibility and philosophical "oomph." Here we briefly survey a few alternative proof systems that score better on these fronts.

8.5.1 Fitch Systems

For relevance logics, the best known alternatives to Hilbert systems are Fitch systems. In fact, Fitch systems and Fitch-system proofs are mentioned in the opening pages of Anderson and Belnap (1975) already, and are appealed to repeatedly throughout that text. Another Fitch system that is fairly well known is the system in Mares (2004). A comprehensive overview of Fitch systems for a broad family of relevance logics can be found in Brady (1984b), which is where we will focus most of our attention.

A key idea in these systems is the importation of tools for directly tracking the *use* of premises in a deduction. To do this, formulas in a derivation are labeled with a set of numbers that very loosely track which other formulas have been *used* in the derivation to that point. For the sake of brevity, we will also restrict our attention to the rules governing the conditional. As an example, the conditional-only fragment of Brady's Fitch system for **B** is characterized by (essentially) the following rules:

Hyp. A formula A may be introduced as the hypothesis of a new (sub)derivation with the subscript $\{k\}$, where k is the number of subderivations A occurs in the scope of.

Rep. A_X may be repeated in the same subderivation, retaining its index set X.

Reit. A_X may be reiterated into any subderivation inside the subderivation containing A_X, retaining the index set X.

$\to I$ From a derivation of B_X on the hypothesis $A_{\{k\}}$, infer $A \to B_{X-\{k\}}$, provided $k \in X$, closing the subderivation.

$\to E$ From A_X and $A \to B_Y$, infer $B_{X \cup Y}$, provided either $Y = \emptyset$ or $X = \{m\}$ and max $Y < m$.

The restrictions on $\to I$ and $\to E$ both deserve justification. Probably the *very best* way to provide such justification would be by providing a completeness proof. We don't have the space for that, so we'll instead just demonstrate a few failed derivations that (a) we are glad to see fail, given that our target logic is **B**, and (b) whose failure is facilitated by the restrictions.

First up, let's see why $A \to B \vdash (B \to C) \to (A \to C)$ fails. Intuitively, one expects to prove this by first assuming $A \to B$, then assuming $B \to C$ in a new subderivation, then assuming A in yet another subderivation, deriving C in said subderivation, then applying $\to I$ several times. Attempting this, one gets this far before running into problems:

$$
\begin{array}{lll}
1 & A \to B_{\{1\}} & \text{Hyp.} \\
2 & B \to C_{\{2\}} & \text{Hyp.} \\
3 & A_{\{3\}} & \text{Hyp.} \\
4 & B_{\{1,3\}} & \to E\ 1,3 \\
5 & C_? & ??? \\
\end{array}
$$

The issue at this point is that $2 < \max\{1,3\}$. So the restriction on the application of the $\to E$ rule prevents the derivation of C in the innermost subderivation here. The reader will be able to easily verify that essentially the same problem prevents the derivation of $B \to C \vdash (A \to B) \to (A \to C)$.

The use of the strict inequality "<" is also crucial. To see why, note that were we to replace the "<" with "≤," the following would be a derivation of $A \to B, A \vdash B$:

$$
\begin{array}{r|ll}
1 & A \to B_{\{1\}} & \\
2 & A_{\{1\}} & \text{Hyp.} \\
3 & B_{\{1\}} & \to E \text{ modified}
\end{array}
$$

Finally, to see what motivates the restriction placed on $\to I$, suppose again that the restriction *isn't* in place and note that we could then give the following derivation of $A \vdash B \to A$:

$$
\begin{array}{r|ll}
1 & A_{\{1\}} & \text{Hyp.} \\
2 & \quad B_{\{2\}} & \text{Hyp.} \\
3 & \quad A_{\{1\}} & \text{Reit.} \\
4 & B \to A_{\{2\}} & \to I \text{ modified}
\end{array}
$$

But clearly this is also something we need to avoid in **B**.

Logics stronger than **B** have Fitch systems where different restrictions on these rules are in play. Altogether, there is a rich and interesting family of proof systems here, and they are less philosophically well explored than (to my eyes) it seems they ought to be. Interested readers are encouraged to investigate!

8.5.2 Bunched Systems

The most obviously proof-theoretic of the options we'll survey are the bunched systems usually associated with the work of Stephen Read, since they form the basis of the system he presented in Read (1988). The basic idea is to mimic in our proof theory the pair of operations we use to interpret the semantics. Thus, rather than using one premise-combining operation expressed with a comma, bunched systems allow two distinct premise-combining operations – with one typically expressed with a comma and the other with a semicolon.

Intuitively, one of these operations – following Read, we'll say the comma – is to be read as the "union" operation and the other (in our case, the semicolon) is to be read as the application operation. (This choice is, unfortunately, not uniform across the folks working in this general area. In fact, the divide is roughly disciplinary, with philosophers and philosophically minded logicians largely adhering to the preceding convention and computer scientists largely switching things the other way around.) What this means is that a bunched sequent of the form "$X, Y \succ A$" will mean that any point that verifies both X and Y will also verify A, while a bunched sequent of the form "$X; Y \succ A$" will mean "applying a point that verifies X to a point that verifies Y results in a point that verifies A."

How this matters: consider conjunction first. A typical sequent-style conjunction introduction rule has the following form:

$$\frac{X \succ B \qquad Y \succ C}{X, Y \succ B \wedge C} \ .$$

Given our interpretation of the comma as the union-esque premise-combining operation, this seems like a plausible rule. After all, if points that verify X verify B and points that verify Y verify C, then if we've got on hand a point that verifies both X and Y, then what we've got on hand is also a point that verifies both B and C. So it's a point that verifies $B \wedge C$.

On the other hand, if we switch all the commas to semicolons, the result is a rule that seems deeply implausible:

$$\frac{X \succ B \qquad Y \succ C}{X; Y \succ B \wedge C} \ .$$

Recalling that the semicolon is meant to pick out the premise-combining operation corresponding to the application operation, there is no good reason to expect points that verify $X; Y$ to have anything to do with either B or C, let alone with $B \wedge C$. After all, when we apply a point verifying X to a point verifying Y, the result is a point that verifies the consequent of every conditional verified in the first point that has an antecedent verified in the second point. Thus, in the preceding situation, we could only infer that $B \wedge C$ is verified in the point in question if we had some reason to think that every point verifying B also verified $C \rightarrow (B \wedge C)$ – that is just if we have reason to think that $B \rightarrow (C \rightarrow (B \wedge C))$ is a theorem of the logic in question. But we saw in Section 3 that this is not a theorem of **B**.

For the conditional, the matter is reversed – the semicolon-y version of the usual conditional elimination rule is quite plausible:

$$\frac{X \succ A \rightarrow B \qquad Y \succ A}{X; Y \succ B} \ .$$

This is, after all, the behavior we've come to expect of application. If we replace the semicolon with the comma, though, the resulting rule should fail in logics where conjunctive syllogism is off the table. After all, if X gets me $A \rightarrow B$ and Y gets me A, the best I can expect to get from the union of X and Y – which is to say from X, Y – is $(A \rightarrow B) \wedge A$. Without something in the neighborhood of conjunctive syllogism, this just doesn't suffice for B.

There's much more to be said about bunched proof systems, but the preceding discussion should give the reader an intuitive feel for how they end up being used in relevant logics. Bunched systems have also seen extensive investigation in theoretical computer science – see, for example, Pym (2013).

8.5.3 Concluding Thoughts

These alternatives provide ways for us to study relevant logics using more philosophically perspicuous proof systems. But they aren't the only alternatives available. For space reasons, we will not give even a cursory survey of any further alternatives. But we would be remiss if we do not at least *mention* work on display calculi (see e.g. Belnap [1982] or Restall [1998]) which has been seen to have interesting connections to the gaggle theoretic machinery that was mentioned earlier – see Restall (1995) for details.

8.6 Richer Vocabulary

Another natural family of extensions are the extensions that use richer vocabulary. In the preceding discussion we examined a propositional language and a first-order language. But logics containing richer and more varied vocabulary can be studied from a relevant perspective as well. Here we'll briefly discuss three options in this vein: modal relevant logics, relevant justification logics, and dynamic relevant logics.

8.6.1 Modality

As with the rest of the story we've told in this Element, our treatment of modality is inspired by the treatment found in Fine (1974). First, the basics: rather than following Kripke (see Kripke [1963]) in interpreting modality using a binary relation R, we instead interpret it using a unary operation that I'll write as "u." Intuitively, where t is a theory, $u(t)$ is the theory that spells out the theory of necessity at work in t. I'll call u "the unboxing" function because in the canonical model, the function that interprets u is the function $t \mapsto \{A : \Box A \in t\}$.

As with the binary application operation, so also the unary unboxing operation ceases to be well-defined if we restrict our attention to primes – $\Box(A \vee B)$ doesn't (and shouldn't!) entail $\Box A \vee \Box B$. Even in *classical* modal logics, this fails, since classical modal logics typically contain $\Box(A \vee \neg A)$ for all A, but for some A, fail to contain either $\Box A$ or $\Box \neg A$. Thus there are prime theories that do contain $\Box(A \vee B)$ and don't contain $\Box A \vee \Box B$, and thus don't contain $\Box A$ and don't contain $\Box B$. But obviously the unboxing of such a theory is not prime.

Formally, models for modally extended **B** are given by adding the previously mentioned "unboxing" function u to the definition of a model. If we require no more than monotonicity of u (so that if $s \sqsubseteq t$, then $u(s) \sqsubseteq u(t)$) and interpret the necessity operator by the following clause:

$$t \vDash \Box B \text{ iff } u(t) \vDash B,$$

then the resulting set of validities is captured by the axioms and rules of **B** (in the extended language) together with the following rule and axiom:

- $\dfrac{A \to B}{\Box A \to \Box B}$
- $(\Box A \wedge \Box B) \to \Box(A \wedge B)$.

To ensure the semantics verifies other desirable modal postulates, one puts further restrictions on the behavior of the unboxing function. For example,

- To validate all instances of $\Box A \to A$, we require that $u(t) \sqsubseteq t$;
- To validate all instances of $\Box A \to \Box \Box A$, we require that $u(t) \sqsubseteq u(u(t))$;
- To validate all instances of $\Box(A \to B) \to (\Box A \to \Box B)$, we require that $u(s) \circ u(t) \sqsubseteq u(s \circ t)$; and
- To ensure closure under the rule $\dfrac{A}{\Box A}$, we require that $\ell \sqsubseteq u(\ell)$.

The "functional" perspective on modality casts Kripke semantics in an interesting light. The following loose simile roughly explains why: Kripke's binary-relational semantics for $\Box$ is to the preceding functional semantics for $\Box$ as the ternary relational semantics for $\to$ is to the binary relational semantics for $\to$. The simile isn't perfect, but comparing the two approaches to the latter pieces of vocabulary provides impetus for a variety of ways of rethinking semantics for modals that are worth taking a good hard look at.

8.6.2 Justification Logics

We can also generalize the preceding approach as follows. Instead of augmenting the propositional vocabulary with modals that model the behavior of the unary connective "necessarily," we can instead add modals that model the behavior of unary connectives of the form "t justifies" where "t" can (and generally does) vary. To capture this, we extend our language with a family of justification *terms*, and for each justification term t, a justification modal $[\![t]\!]$.

From my perspective, the interesting bits in justification logics concern how justifications combine. As an example, if t justifies $A \to B$ and s justifies A, then one expects that t and s can be combined to justify B and can also be combined to justify $(A \to B) \wedge A$. But, for reasons that by this point in the Element should be clear, one expects that these methods of combining justifications will be distinct. So we might expect there to be both "union-like" and "application like" operations on justifications ($\sqcup$ and $\cdot$, respectively) and that, in terms of these, the expectations we just enunciated can be cashed out as follows:

$$([\![t]\!](A \to B) \wedge [\![s]\!]A) \to [\![t \cdot s]\!]B,$$
$$([\![t]\!](A \to B) \wedge [\![s]\!]A) \to [\![t \sqcup s]\!]((A \to B) \wedge A).$$

Of course, having presented it this way, questions that blend technical and philosophical matters immediately rear their heads. First: is conjunction really the correct way to combine the premises in both cases? Given that "$\cdot$" is meant to model application of one justification to another, one might think that what it takes to infer $[\![t \cdot s]\!]B$ is something that forces application on us – for example, perhaps it should be a "fusion"-like connective or an outright entailment. Second: our preferred semantic story interprets points in models as theories. But what does it even mean for a theory to contain or otherwise demonstrate some claim about justifications? What, for that matter, *are* theory-relative justifications?

Work in this area is in its infancy, so the preceding questions are not only unaddressed, they are mostly unarticulated in the relevant context. The reader looking for further information is directed to Savic and Studer (2019) and Standefer (2022a), which are good starting points.

8.6.3 Concluding Thoughts and Other Extensions

There are, of course, other interesting ways we might extend our vocabulary. Here we briefly (and, again, non-exhaustively) mention just these:

Dynamic logics, like justification logics, augment our vocabulary with a range of modal operators $[\![t]\!]$. But intuitively, where justification logics take "$[\![t]\!]A$" to record that t justifies A, dynamic logics instead take "$[\![B]\!]$" to record that the operation/action t results in A. Despite these philosophical differences, justification logics and dynamic logics remain quite similar at the level of their formalisms. We encourage interested readers to consult the original work by Sylvan on the subject (see Sylvan [1992]) or the very recent work by Tedder and Bilková (see Tedder and Bilková [2022]).

We might add an identity predicate. This has been explored in Mares (1992), Kremer (1999), and Standefer (2021) among other places.

Instead of first-order (object) quantifiers we might add higher-order *propositional* quantifiers. This was already on the table in Anderson and Belnap (1975), and had already been studied semantically in Routley and Meyer (1972a). Further important results can be found in Kremer (1993) and Goldblatt and Kane (2010).

We might aim to model the language of arithmetic, preferably in such a way that the resulting systems in some way model arithmetic itself. A special issue of the *Australasian Journal of Logic* has been recently devoted to this; see Ferguson and Priest (2021). The papers there present both the state of the art and an overview of the history of the subject. On the latter front, the papers of Robert Meyer and Chris Mortensen included there are of particular import; see Meyer (2021c), Meyer (2021a), Meyer (2021b) and Meyer and Mortensen (2021b), Meyer and Mortensen (2021a), and Mortensen (2021). The most pressing of the open problems in the area are, however, addressed in Friedman and Meyer (1992).

We could combine the modal extension discussed previously with the quantified extension examined in the previous section. This has been examined a few times, especially by Nick Ferenz – see, for example, Ferenz (2022).

8.7 Yet More

None of the preceding examinations exhaust their respective domains. If they did, they still wouldn't exhaust the scope of current ongoing research on relevance logics. To get slightly (though only very slightly) closer, I'll close the section by listing a few further areas that are seeing ongoing, active research:

Relevant predication and relevant connectives: there's been some research on what it means to *relevantly* predicate some property of an object. The starting point for such investigations is with the work of Dunn in Dunn (1987), Dunn (1990b), Dunn (1990c), and Dunn (1990a). But Dunn is not the only one to have worked on the issue. In this vein, the work of Kremer cannot go unmentioned; see, for example, Kremer (1989) and Kremer (1997). A somewhat similar line of questioning concerns what it takes for a *connective* to be relevant. Here there's been much less work, and to my knowledge the only published work explicitly devoted to the topic is Standefer (2022b).

There are also logics stronger than **R** that mimic various properties of relevance logics. Of special note in this are the logic **RM** long championed by Dunn (see, for example, Dunn [1970] and Dunn [1976]; a decent history of **RM** can be found in Dunn [2021]) and the logic **KR** that was advocated for by Kerr (see Kerr [2021]).

The theory-building framework I've pursued throughout this Element is inspired by Jc Beall's work on the topic. Beall, however, takes this approach to lead to a different place – namely, to the logic known as **FDE**. For more on Beall's work, the reader is referred to Beall (2017) and Beall (2018). For the connections between Beall's approach and **FDE** and the approach taken here, see Logan (2022a). For the range of different places Beall's approach might lead and for discussion of whether one of these is "the right" place to go, see Beall and Logan (2017) and Beall and Restall (2005).

More generally, there's been a great deal of work on what are known as substructural logics. These are logics that reject certain so-called "structural rules" accepted by classical logic. Greg Restall has been particularly influential in the philosophical investigation of these logics, and his textbook Restall (2000) is an invaluable resource for philosophical logicians looking to break into this area. Also worth mentioning is the somewhat orthogonal but also plausibly substructural work recently being produced in the intellectual circles surrounding the Buenos Aires Logic Group – see, for example, Barrio, Pailos, and Szmuc (2020).

Relevant logics weaker than our preferred logic **B** have also seen some recent interest. The central object of investigation here tends to be the logic known as **BB**, which was studied by Peter Lavers (1985, 1994) and has seen a bit of recent interest as well – see, for example, Tedder (2021). **BB** differs from **B** as follows: in place of the conjunction introduction and disjunction elimination *axioms* (viz. A3 and A5 in our numbering) they instead use the following conjunction introduction and disjunction elimination *rules*:

$$\frac{A \to B \quad A \to C}{A \to (B \land C)} \qquad \frac{A \to C \quad B \to C}{(A \lor B) \to C}.$$

But while **BB** has been the focus of most of the work on relevant logics weaker than **B**, both Tedder and Lavers have introduced, motivated, and studied logics that are weaker yet. Other folks have studied further ways of weakening logics – up to and including rejection of the identity axiom $A \to A$ – see, for example, French (2016) for a relevance-friendly account of such rejection.

Another toolkit that I regret not having room to discuss in this Element is the metavaluational toolkit. Metavaluations combine both semantical and proof-theoretical machinery into one rather surprisingly effective package. They were introduced by R. K. Meyer (1976) and have turned out to be among the most useful tools in the relevant logicians toolbox. Brady (2017a) presents an overview of a variety of these uses and contains references to a large fragment of the literature in which metavaluations occur.

Finally, there's been some study – chiefly by Stephen Read – of the extent to which relevant logics are a truly novel phenomenon. In his Read (1988), for example, Read puts some work into connecting relevance to matters raised already by medieval logicians. He has returned to this thread elsewhere as well; see, for example, Read (1993).

The field contains more than is mentioned here and is wide open for even further options. My hope is that the reader who has made it to this point is well-equipped to explore these or other avenues productively.

References

Anderson, A. R., & Belnap, N. D. (1975). *Entailment: The logic of relevance and necessity, vol. I*. Princeton University Press.

Anderson, A. R., Belnap, N. D., & Dunn, J. M. (1992). *Entailment: The logic of relevance and necessity, vol. II*. Princeton University Press.

Atwood, M. (2006). *The handmaid's tale*. Everyman's Library.

Barrio, E. A., Pailos, F., & Szmuc, D. (2020). A hierarchy of classical and paraconsistent logics. *Journal of Philosophical Logic, 49*(1), 93–120.

Beall, J. (2017). There is no logical negation: True, false, both, and neither. *Australasian Journal of Logic, 14*(1), Article no. 1.

Beall, J. (2018). The simple argument for subclassical logic. *Philosophical Issues, 28*(1), 30–54.

Beall, J. (2019). FDE as the one true logic. In *New essays on Belnap–Dunn logic* (pp. 115–125). Springer.

Beall, J., & Logan, S. A. (2017). *Logic: The basics (2nd edition)*. Routledge.

Beall, J., & Restall, G. (2005). *Logical pluralism*. Oxford University Press.

Belnap, N. D. (1960). Entailment and relevance. *The Journal of Symbolic Logic, 25*(2), 144–146.

Belnap, N. D. (1982). Display logic. *Journal of Philosophical Logic, 11*(4), 375–417. doi: https://doi.org/10.1007/bf00284976.

Bennett, J. (1969). Entailment. *The Philosophical Review, 78*(2), 197–236.

Berto, F., & Restall, G. (2019). Negation on the Australian plan. *Journal of Philosophical Logic, 48*(6), 1119–1144. doi: https://doi.org/10.1007/s10992-019-09510-2.

Bimbó, K. (2007). Relevance logics. In D. Jacquette (Ed.), *Handbook of the philosophy of science: Philosophy of logic*. North-Holland Academic Publishers.

Bimbó, K., & Dunn, J. M. (2008). *Generalized Galois logics: Relational semantics of nonclassical logical calculi*. Center for the Study of Language and Information.

Brady, R. T. (1984a). Depth relevance of some paraconsistent logics. *Studia Logica, 43*(1), 63–73.

Brady, R. T. (1984b). Natural deduction systems for some quantified relevant logics. *Logique et Analyse, 27*(108), 355–378.

Brady, R. T. (1988). A content semantics for quantified relevant logics I. *Studia Logica, 47*(2), 111–127.

Brady, R. T. (1989). A content semantics for quantified relevant logics II. *Studia Logica, 48*(2), 243–257.

Brady, R. T. (2006). *Universal logic.* CSLI Publications.

Brady, R. T. (2017a). Metavaluations. *Bulletin of Symbolic Logic, 23*(3), 296–323.

Brady, R. T. (2017b). Some concerns regarding ternary-relation semantics and truth-theoretic semantics in general. *IfCoLog Journal of Logics and Their Applications, 4*(3), 755–781.

Brauer, E. (2020). Relevance for the classical logician. *The Review of Symbolic Logic, 13*(2), 436–457.

Carroll, L. (1895). What the tortoise said to Achilles. *Mind, 4*(14), 278–280.

Copeland, B. J. (1979). On when a semantics is not a semantics: Some reasons for disliking the Routley-Meyer semantics for relevance logic. *Journal of Philosophical Logic, 8*(1), 399–413.

Copeland, B. J. (1980). The trouble Anderson and Belnap have with relevance. *Philosophical Studies, 37*(4), 325–334.

Dunn, J. M. (1970). Algebraic completeness results for R-mingle and its extensions. *The Journal of Symbolic Logic, 35*(1), 1–13.

Dunn, J. M. (1976). A Kripke-style semantics for R-mingle using a binary accessibility relation. *Studia Logica: An International Journal for Symbolic Logic, 35*(2), 163–172.

Dunn, J. M. (1987). Relevant predication 1: The formal theory. *Journal of Philosophical Logic, 16*(4), 347–381.

Dunn, J. M. (1990a). The frame problem and relevant predication. In *Knowledge representation and defeasible reasoning* (pp. 89–95). Springer.

Dunn, J. M. (1990b). Relevant predication 2: Intrinsic properties and internal relations. *Philosophical Studies, 60*(3), 177–206.

Dunn, J. M. (1990c). Relevant predication 3: Essential properties. In *Truth or consequences* (pp. 77–95). Springer.

Dunn, J. M. (1993). Star and perp: Two treatments of negation. *Philosophical Perspectives, 7*, 331–357.

Dunn, J. M. (2021). R-Mingle is nice, and so is Arnon Avron. In *Arnon Avron on semantics and proof theory of non-classical logics* (pp. 141–165). Springer.

Ferenz, N. (2022). Quantified modal relevant logics. *The Review of Symbolic Logic, 16*(1), 210–240.

Ferenz, N., & Tedder, A. (2022). Neighbourhood semantics for modal relevant logics. *Journal of Philosophical Logic, 52*, 145–181.

Ferguson, T. M., & Priest, G. (Eds.). (2021). Special issue on Robert Meyer and relevant arithmetic. *The Australasian Journal of Logic, 18*(5).

Fine, K. (1974). Models for entailment. *Journal of Philosophical Logic, 3*(4), 347–372.

Fine, K. (1988). Semantics for quantified relevance logic. *Journal of Philosophical Logic, 17*(1), 27–59.

Fine, K. (1989). Incompleteness for quantified relevance logics. In *Directions in relevant logic* (pp. 205–225). Springer.

Fitting, M., & Mendelsohn, R. L. (2012). *First-order modal logic* (Vol. 277). Springer Science & Business Media.

French, R. (2016). Structural reflexivity and the paradoxes of self-reference. *Ergo, an Open Access Journal of Philosophy, 3*. doi: http://doi.org/10.39 98/ergo.12405314.0003.005

Friedman, H., & Meyer, R. (1992). Whither relevant arithmetic? *The Journal of Symbolic Logic, 57*(3), 824–831.

Goble, L. (2003). Neighborhoods for entailment. *Journal of Philosophical Logic, 32*(5), 483–529. doi: https://doi.org/10.1023/a:1025638012192.

Gödel, K. (1932). Zum intuitionistischen aussagenkalkül. *Anzeiger der Akademie der Wissenschaften in Wien, 69*, 65–66.

Goldblatt, R., & Kane, M. (2010). An admissible semantics for propositionally quantified relevant logics. *Journal of Philosophical Logic, 39*(1), 73–100.

Hanson, W. H. (1989). Two kinds of deviance. *History and Philosophy of Logic, 10*(1), 15–28. doi: https://doi.org/10.1080/01445348908837139.

Harrop, R. (1960). Concerning formulas of the types $a \to (b \lor c)$, $a \to \exists x b(x)$ in intuitionistic formal systems. *The Journal of Symbolic Logic, 25*(1), 27–32.

Humberstone, I. (1988). Operational semantics for positive R. *Notre Dame Journal of Formal Logic, 29*(1), 61–80.

Kerr, A. D. (2021). A plea for KR. *Synthese, 198*(4), 3047–3071.

Kremer, P. (1989). Relevant predication: Grammatical characterisations. *Journal of Philosophical Logic, 18*(4), 349–382.

Kremer, P. (1993). Quantifying over propositions in relevance logic: Nonaxiomatisability of primary interpretations of $\forall p$ and $\exists p$. *The Journal of Symbolic Logic, 58*(1), 334–349.

Kremer, P. (1997). Dunn's relevant predication, real properties and identity. *Erkenntnis, 47*(1), 37–65.

Kremer, P. (1999). Relevant identity. *Journal of Philosophical Logic, 28*(2), 199–222.

Kripke, S. A. (1963). Semantical considerations on modal logic. *Acta Philosophica Fennica, 16*, 83–94.

Lavers, P. (1985). Generating intensional logics (unpublished master's thesis). University of Adelaide.

Lavers, P. (1994). Generalising tautological entailment. *Logique et Analyse,* *37*(147/148), 367–377.

Logan, S. A. (2019). Notes on stratified semantics. *Journal of Philosophical Logic, 48*(4), 749–786.

Logan, S. A. (2021). Strong depth relevance. *Australasian Journal of Logic, 18*(6), 645–656.

Logan, S. A. (2022a). Deep fried logic. *Erkenntnis, 87*(1), 257–286. doi: https://doi.org/10.1007/s10670-019-00194-3.

Logan, S. A. (2022b). Depth relevance and hyperformalism. *Journal of Philosophical Logic, 51*(4):721–737.

Logan, S. A., & Leach-Krouse, G. (2021). On not saying what we shouldn't have to say. *The Australasian Journal of Logic, 18*(5), 524–568.

Mares, E. D. (1992). Semantics for relevance logic with identity. *Studia Logica, 51*(1), 1–20.

Mares, E. D. (2004). *Relevant logic: A philosophical interpretation.* Cambridge University Press.

Mares, E. D., & Goldblatt, R. (2006). An alternative semantics for quantified relevant logic. *The Journal of Symbolic Logic, 71*(1), 163–187.

Méndez, J. M., & Robles, G. (2012). A general characterization of the variable-sharing property by means of logical matrices. *Notre Dame Journal of Formal Logic, 53*(2), 223–244.

Meyer, R. (2021a). Arithmetic formulated relevantly. *The Australasian Journal of Logic, 18*(5), 154–288.

Meyer, R. (2021b). The consistency of arithmetic. *The Australasian Journal of Logic, 18*(5), 289–379.

Meyer, R. (2021c). Relevant arithmetic. *The Australasian Journal of Logic, 18*(5), 150–153.

Meyer, R., & Mortensen, C. (202a). Alien intruders in relevant arithmetic. *The Australasian Journal of Logic, 18*(5), 401–425.

Meyer, R., & Mortensen, C. (2021b). Inconsistent models for relevant arithmetics. *The Australasian Journal of Logic, 18*(5), 380–400.

Meyer, R. K. (1976). Metacompleteness. *Notre Dame Journal of Formal Logic, 17*(4), 501–516.

Mortensen, C. (2021). Remark on relevant arithmetic. *The Australasian Journal of Logic, 18*(5), 426–427.

Padro, R. (2015). What the tortoise said to Kripke: The adoption problem and the epistemology of logic (unpublished doctoral dissertation). City University of New York.

Pym, D. (2013). *The semantics and proof theory of the logic of bunched implications.* Springer Netherlands.

Read, S. (1988). *Relevant logic: A philosophical examination of inference.* Blackwell.

Read, S. (1993). Formal and material consequence, disjunctive syllogism and gamma. In *Argumentationstheorie* (pp. 233–259). Brill.

Restall, G. (1995). Display logic and gaggle theory. *Reports on Mathematical Logic*, 133–146.

Restall, G. (1998). Displaying and deciding substructural logics 1: Logics with contraposition. *Journal of Philosophical Logic*, *27*(2), 179–216. doi: https://doi.org/10.1023/a:1017998605966.

Restall, G. (1999). Negation in relevant logics (how I stopped worrying and learned to love the Routley star). In D. M. Gabbay & H. Wansing (Eds.), *What is negation?* (pp. 53–76). Kluwer Academic Publishers.

Restall, G. (2000). *An introduction to substructural logics.* Routledge.

Restall, G., & Standefer, S. (2022). Collection frames for distributive substructural logics. *The Review of Symbolic Logic*, *16*(4):1120–1157

Robles, G., & Méndez, J. M. (2014). Generalizing the depth relevance condition: Deep relevant logics not included in R-mingle. *Notre Dame Journal of Formal Logic*, *55*(1), 107–127.

Robles, G., & Méndez, J. M. (2018). *Routley-Meyer ternary relational semantics for intuitionistic-type negations.* Academic Press.

Routley, R., & Meyer, R. K. (1972a). The semantics of entailment. In H. Leblanc (Ed.), (pp. 199–243). North-Holland Publishing Company.

Routley, R., & Meyer, R. K. (1972b). The semantics of entailment II. *Journal of Philosophical Logic*, *1*(1), 53–73.

Routley, R., & Meyer, R. K. (1972c). The semantics of entailment III. *Journal of Philosophical Logic*, *1*(2), 192–208.

Routley, R., & Meyer, R. K. (1975a). Towards a general semantical theory of implication and conditionals. II. Systems with normal conjunctions and disjunctions and aberrant and normal negations. *Reports on Mathematical Logic* (9), 47–62.

Routley, R., & Meyer, R. K. (1975b). Towards a general semantical theory of implication and conditionals. I. Systems with normal conjunctions and disjunctions and aberrant and normal negations. *Reports on Mathematical Logic* (4), 67–89.

Routley, R., Plumwood, V., Meyer, R. K., & Brady, R. T. (1982). In R. Sylvan & R. Brady (Eds.), *Relevant logics and their rivals.* Ridgeview.

Routley, R., & Routley, V. (1972). The semantics of first degree entailment. *Noûs*, 335–359.

Savic, N., & Studer, T. (2019). Relevant justification logic. *Journal of Applied Logics*, *6*(2), 395–410.

Slaney, J. (1984). A metacompleteness theorem for contraction-free relevant logics. *Studia Logica, 43*(1), 159–168.

Slaney, J. (1990). A general logic. *Australasian Journal of Philosophy, 68*(1), 74–88.

Slaney, J. (1995). *MaGIC: Matrix generator for implication connectives* (Tech. Rep.). Tech. Report TR-ARP-11-95, Research School of Information Science.

Standefer, S. (2019). Tracking reasons with extensions of relevant logics. *Logic Journal of the IGPL, 27*(4), 543–569. doi: https://doi.org/10.1093/jigpal/jzz018.

Standefer, S. (2021). Identity in Mares–Goldblatt models for quantified relevant logic. *Journal of Philosophical Logic, 50*(6), 1389–1415.

Standefer, S. (2022a). Weak relevant justification logics. *Journal of Logic and Computation, 33*(7):1665–1683.

Standefer, S. (2022b). What is a relevant connective? *Journal of Philosophical Logic, 51*(4), 919–950. doi: https://doi.org/10.1007/s10992-022-09655-7.

Sylvan, R. (1992). Process and action: Relevant theory and logics. *Studia Logica, 51*(3), 379–437.

Szmuc, D. E. (2021). The (greatest) fragment of classical logic that respects the variable-sharing principle (in the FMLA-FMLA framework). *Bulletin of the Section of Logic, 50*(4), 421–453.

Tedder, A. (2021). Information flow in logics in the vicinity of BB. *The Australasian Journal of Logic, 18*(1), 1–24.

Tedder, A., & Bilková, M. (2022). Relevant propositional dynamic logic. *Synthese, 200*(3), 1–42.

Tedder, A., & Ferenz, N. (2022). Neighbourhood semantics for quantified relevant logics. *Journal of Philosophical Logic, 51*(3), 457–484.

Urquhart, A. (1972). Semantics for relevant logics. *Journal of Symbolic Logic, 37*(1), 159–169. doi: https://doi.org/10.2307/2272559.

Acknowledgments

Lots and lots of folks deserve thanks. First up are Kim, Terry, and Carrie. Thanks for tolerating me even when working on this Element made me grouchy. Next up are Blane, Graham, and Joe. Our jam sessions in my office were inspirational and pushed me to fight the good fight when I really would've rather just, like, not. Also crucial, in a different way, were Tedder, Teresa, and Eileen. You all are fabulous at telling me my bad ideas are bad without ever saying anything like that. The participants in the ESSLLI session I jointly ran with Tedder that covered some of this deserve thanks, but probably also an apology for all the awful jokes. And last of all I'll thank Jc Beall for dragging me through the rewrite of our jointly authored book and giving me the ideas that led to the interpretation I give here, and Stephen Read for patiently letting me fail at writing a book with him, and still, in spite of that, recommending that I write this one.

Cambridge Elements ⹅

Philosophy and Logic

Bradley Armour-Garb
SUNY Albany

Bradley Armour-Garb is chair and Professor of Philosophy at SUNY Albany. His books include *The Law of Non-Contradiction* (co-edited with Graham Priest and J. C. Beall, 2004), *Deflationary Truth* and *Deflationism and Paradox* (both co-edited with J. C. Beall, 2005), *Pretense and Pathology* (with James Woodbridge, Cambridge University Press, 2015), *Reflections on the Liar* (2017), and *Fictionalism in Philosophy* (co-edited with Fred Kroon, 2020).

Frederick Kroon
The University of Auckland

Frederick Kroon is Emeritus Professor of Philosophy at the University of Auckland. He has authored numerous papers in formal and philosophical logic, ethics, philosophy of language, and metaphysics, and is the author of *A Critical Introduction to Fictionalism* (with Stuart Brock and Jonathan McKeown-Green, 2018).

About the Series

This Cambridge Elements series provides an extensive overview of the many and varied connections between philosophy and logic. Distinguished authors provide an up-to-date summary of the results of current research in their fields and give their own take on what they believe are the most significant debates influencing research, drawing original conclusions.

Cambridge Elements ⬮

Philosophy and Logic

Elements in the Series

A full series listing is available at: www.cambridge.org/EPL